Cerys Matthews

HOOK, LINE & SINGER

125 songs to sing out loud

PENGUIN BOOKS

PENGUIN BOOKS

Published by the Penguin Group

Penguin Books Ltd, 80 Strand, London WC2R ORL, England

Penguin Group (USA) Inc., 375 Hudson Street, New York, New York 10014, USA

Penguin Group (Canada), 90 Eglinton Avenue East, Suite 700, Toronto, Ontario, Canada M4P 2Y3
(a division of Pearson Penguin Canada Inc.)

Penguin Ireland, 25 St Stephen's Green, Dublin 2, Ireland
(a division of Penguin Books Ltd)

Penguin Group (Australia), 707 Collins Street, Melbourne, Victoria 3008, Australia
(a division of Pearson Australia Group Pty Ltd)

Penguin Books India Pvt Ltd, 11 Community Centre, Panchsheel Park, New Delhi – 110 017, India

Penguin Group (NZ), 67 Apollo Drive, Rosedale, North Shore 0632, New Zealand
(a division of Pearson New Zealand Ltd)

Penguin Books (South Africa) (Pty) Ltd, Block D, Rosebank Office Park,
181 Jan Smuts Avenue, Parktown North, Gauteng 2193, South Africa

Penguin Books Ltd, Registered Offices: 80 Strand, London WC2R ORL, England

www.penguin.com

First published by Particular Books 2013
Published in Penguin Books 2014

1

Copyright © Cerys Matthews, 2013

The moral right of the author has been asserted

Music set by Julian Elloway

Printed in China

A CIP catalogue record for this book is available from the British Library

978-1-846-14718-0

CONTENTS

5
Let's Go Fly a Kite   110

6
Monoglots to Polyglots   134

7
La, La, La, La, La, l'America   162

8
Sea Dogs and Blue Water   188

Introduction

*'Keep a green tree in your heart and
perhaps a singing bird will come'*

~ CHINESE PROVERB

WE WERE DRIVING along the hedge-bound country lanes of
Pembrokeshire *circa* 1973 in our Vauxhall Viva. There was a tractor ahead
of us, pulling a gargantuan sow in an open trailer. The sow jumped out,
broke her leg and hobbled off with farmer chasing. And what did we do? Of
course, we burst into song — 'Mochyn Du' ('Black Pig') it was, specifically,
a song about a dead pig. Cruel? Yes. And memorable? Yes. It endures as
my earliest memory, and here's why I'm sitting here compiling this book of
songs — life itself supplies you with the best of soundtracks.

And then comes the extra dimension songs bring to your life. They
allow you to step inside another person's shoes, they bridge gaps in time
and place. You may find yourself looking through the eyes of a maiden in
the seventeenth century, or saddled up as a cowboy on a horse roaming the

plains of nineteenth-century Arizona. Songs make places feel real, bring characters to life, and all colours and creeds are represented. Compare this to the more academic tomes mostly focusing on the ruling classes, the religious and the male. In songs you are shoulder to shoulder with the mother, the orphan, the downtrodden, the maimed, the soldier, the butcher, the blacksmith, the sick, the poor, the insane, and you may party hard amongst the night life in the seediest parts of town without risking life or limb ... through songs history becomes very much alive.

As I grew older, my curiosity grew alongside my song collection. I bought books and leaflets, visited local museums, and acquainted myself with singers, historians, artists, record collectors and musicians — and kept learning as many songs as I could. Through them I learned about Ireland's famine and Cajun food; I heard protest songs from Catalonia and sang songs from as far afield as Tarawa, Kenya, Cuba, Trinidad and Australia. After more than thirty years of collecting, I still find there's no better way to spend time than singing along in good company, sharing songs and their stories. So that's the idea of this book. A book to keep handy at home so that when you are caught on the third line of that old song you learned at your friend's aunt's house ... you can look it up and be reminded of the lyrics, its writers, its age and its origins. But more than that, songs are so closely bound with emotions, it might open the door to a truckload of memories too.

The hardest part was which songs to include. Well, it's a singalong book first and foremost, so this is a motley crew of songs which are amongst the most memorable, harrowing or silliest, and amongst the easiest to learn and easiest to sing songs that I know.

I START WITH A CHAPTER FOR YOUNG FAMILIES. I have travelled singlehanded on long-haul flights with two under-three-year-olds. Layovers and delays in airports full of swimming crowds and tired, broken-routined toddlers are a disaster. I know the value of a good song to entertain, to stall a tantrum, to soothe, to distract, to amuse for a moment at least. (Tip for layovers/delays: find an empty-ish gate, put a blanket on the floor and tip out your toys. Other children will join yours and soon you'll have your own little crèche = entertained toddlers and parents for adult conversation and food sharing.) So the songs for the very young are found in the first chapter ('Action Songs'), for one-on-one action activity with your beautiful new baby.

There is a song for every occasion, so there follow a good mood chapter ('If You're Happy and You Know It') and a darker chapter ('Oh Dear, What

Can the Matter Be?'). There are songs for vintage-lovers ('Nana's Tune Emporium'), for trips away ('Let's Go Fly a Kite'), then a multilingual chapter ('Monoglots to Polyglots') and an American chapter ('La, La, La, La, La, L'America'). There's a watery chapter ('Sea Dogs and Blue Water'), 'Creature Songs' for pets and pet-lovers, and songs to soothe ('Sweet Dreams'). Finally there's a chapter of celebration songs ('Christmas and New Year').

Songs are bold, pretty and wild. Yes, wild. They have a life of their own. They will outlive us, travel further than us and touch generations we'll never meet. This sharing and travelling will change them; they might morph into new songs. Take your singing voice, guitar, ukulele, recorder or piano and jump in. The melodies, words and actions are there to assist you, but please change them as you see fit — make them yours.

'EVERYBODY CAN SING!'

So said a vocal coach friend of mine recently.

'But some people are tone deaf, aren't they?' I replied.

'Yes, but they can still enjoy making a noise. It won't trouble them!'

We were making a documentary on Sacred Harp singing (singing songs as loudly as you want from a book called *The Sacred Harp*). Young and old, the religious and non-religious are turning up in droves to these singing meetings the world over. There's no need to be trained, no need to have a sweet voice, and everybody's welcome.

It almost died out (it originated in the 1700s) but is seeing a most amazing surge in popularity. Is there a change in the air? Are we reigniting our love of singing out loud? The joy and elation of a crowd erupting into their favourite song in a stadium has always been there, that soul-stirring camaraderie on the terraces singing your team or country's songs, but on our own we become quite shy:

'Oh, no, I can't sing.'

'My cat can sing better than me.'

'No, don't make me, you'll regret it ...'

'I can't carry a tune, my car could carry a tune better' ... And so on.

But hum ha and la, la, la. People have sung for as long as they've been able to, and doesn't everyone feel better after a good singsong?!

Rewind the clock a minute.

1996. Doctor's office.

'Sit down. How long have you been hoarse?'

'Last few nights.'

'Why do you think it happens?'

'Singing too much, too high. Straining.'

'What do you do to look after your voice?'

'Nothing.'

'OK. I'm going to give you an injection … Lean to your side … There. In an hour you'll notice a difference. You'll be able to do the show. But afterwards rest. No talking. No whispering. Lots of water. Lots of rest.'

'Lots of water, no talking and rest' was the best advice I ever got. Oh, along with this nugget, which Tom Jones whispered to me sometime around 1999, just before a live performance of 'Baby, It's Cold Outside': 'Don't drink alcohol before a show, drink after. You'll sing better, and it'll taste great.'

And that's all the advice I'm giving you, which you won't even need anyways. Although it will come in handy if this book prompts you to embark on a hugely successful sell-out world tour, on a heaven-bound trajectory in the singing world …

But whoa there, horses, for we are not on tour yet, and we won't be singing high-key songs over loud drums endlessly, so we won't inflame our vocal cords or require steroid injections to sing. We won't be talking about diaphragms, head voices, chest voices, nor will we think at all about the technical side of making a noise. We are not going to be singing Handel's *Messiah* or Wagner's 'Ring Cycle'. We are not the marathon runners of opera, we are merely park wanderers. Where possible I've kept to the simplest arrangement for the songs — often in the key of C — so even if you have just started to play the piano, ukelele or guitar, you'll be able to play these songs.

So don't worry.

At all.

Having said that, if you already feel very confident in your capabilities and can't wait to assume your role, take some world-class instruction: get into the 'Jesus' position (stand with your legs shoulder-width apart, your arms slightly raised at your sides, palms open and facing upward). There, courtesy of Shirley Bassey's vocal coach. Now your body is 'open'; you are balanced, relaxed.

Right. If you can make a noise, we're in.

CHAPTER I

Action
Songs

*'The total person sings,
not just the vocal chords'*

~ ESTHER BRONER

'NOT BEING ABLE TO SLEEP during the last months of pregnancy is nature's way of preparing you for the sleep deprivation lying ahead' — now that's a fine example of womankind's capacity for self-delusion. Another corker of positive thinking comes from a second midwife who told me, cheerily: 'A night's sleep is counted as a full night if the baby sleeps from twelve to five a.m.' Eventually you may get used to not sleeping, or start sleeping with one eye open or, even better, the little one will learn to sleep for more than five hours at a time — things do improve. The baby starts to look at you, albeit with the same gooey, loving look they use eyeing up a cardboard box. And when you're facing this smiling, burping, more cognisant kind of living pink blobness, you may feel like singing to it. This first chapter is mainly filled with songs perfect for those one-on-one moments with a young baby. Metamorphosis and repetition is the name of the game. You turn the baby into a rocket, you become a horse, you can both become rowing boats, climb with spiders or go shopping without even leaving the bedroom … and then you get to do it again. And again. And again.

Wind the Bobbin Up

A FABULOUS example of how songs travel: this traditional song originated in Yorkshire in the late 1800s, but it was in America that we picked it up. My daughter, Glenys, learned it at her nursery, where it was sung in a strong Southern drawl. (That drawl is not obligatory.)

The song always takes me back to one particular Nashville summer, a long, slow August when the temperature refused to dip below 104. For over four dusty weeks we sweltered under the dry landlocked skies. Hot days like these would always end in 'water time' at Holly Street Daycare. Passing by, you'd hear squeals of delight as water misted out over thirty diaper-wearing toddlers. I would have done pretty much anything to join those children that summer.

ACTIONS

This was originally a kind of tug-of-war game involving the winding of fists and the tugging of elbows. It has evolved into a more peaceful pastime. Make a winding action with your hands, then a pulling action, then clap as per the lyrics. A stout pointing to the ceiling and the floor, a window and a door keeps this song popular with the little ones.

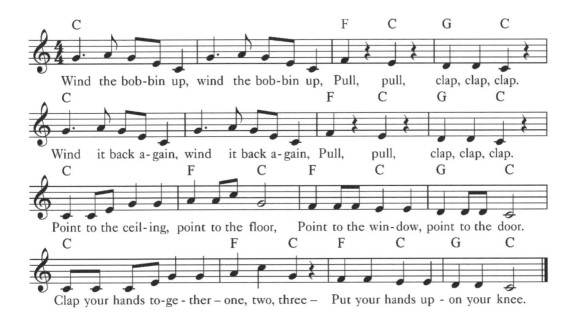

Wind the bobbin up, wind the bobbin up,
Pull, pull, clap, clap, clap.
Wind it back again, wind it back again,
Pull, pull, clap, clap, clap.
Point to the ceiling, point to the floor,
Point to the window, point to the door.
Clap your hands together – one, two, three –
Put your hands upon your knee.

Zoom, Zoom, Zoom

THIS MUST have been written relatively recently because of its subject matter, but the author(s) have already been lost in time and space. Ahem. I came across it when Red kept putting his hands in front of him as if praying to invisible idols. I had no idea what he was doing until I picked him up from nursery one day and the whole room was singing this song. Then it all made sense.

ACTIONS

You do indeed put your hands in front of you, but you are making them your 'rocket' and you 'fly' them up to the moon. When you blast off, launch your 'rocket' upwards.

Alternatively you may use your baby as a rocket by holding them around the waist and hoisting them around in the air in front of you as you sing the first lines. When you get to the 'blast off' bit, launch your baby as high as your arms allow. Don't let go.

OPTION

At the end of the song, say the following lines in a rhythmic, talking-blues kind of way, and it'll lead you back to the start again:

> If you want to take a trip,
> Climb on board my rocket ship.

Zoom, zoom, zoom,
We're going to the moon.
Zoom, zoom, zoom,
We're gonna get there soon.
Ten, nine, eight, seven, six,
    five, four, three, two, one ...
BLAST OFF!

Two Little Dickie Birds

AHA! A song to teach your little ones the art of deception.

According to the Opies' wonderful *Oxford Dictionary of Nursery Rhymes* (1951), the young have been mystified by this sleight of hand for well over two hundred years. The birds' names have changed during this time – they were originally called Jack and Jill, but became the apostles Peter and Paul during the religiously conscientious nineteenth century.

ACTIONS

My mum used to stick a bit of paper on to each of her index fingernails with spit, but you can mark your fingers with a pen or any way you feel like. Wriggle the two marked index fingers in front of you and your 'audience' as you sing the first four lines (keep the rest of your fingers folded away). Then when you sing, 'Fly away, Peter!', tuck your right hand behind your back, fold away your marked finger and unfold your unmarked middle finger, and bring it to the front so you are now wriggling it in front of their eyes. Repeat with your left-hand fingers when you sing, 'Fly away, Paul!' The marked fingers have miraculously disappeared! Then when you sing, 'Come back, Peter!', swap the right-hand fingers back again behind your back, bringing the marked index finger back to the fore, and repeat with the left hand when you sing, 'Come back, Paul!' Just like that. Magic.

Two little dickie birds,
Sitting on a wall;
One named Peter,
One named Paul.
Fly away, Peter!
Fly away, Paul!
Come back, Peter!
Come back, Paul!

Row, Row, Row Your Boat

THIS AMERICAN song was first published in 1852, and may have been born out of the minstrel shows of the 1800s. It can be sung as a round.

You may find yourself becoming very philosophical when singing this song, pondering its deeper meaning. Take a look at 'A Boat Beneath a Sunny Sky' by Lewis Carroll, which ends:

> Ever drifting down the stream –
> Lingering in the golden gleam –
> Life, what is it but a dream?

ACTIONS

Just sit on the floor, facing your partner, with your legs out in front. Hold each other's hands, and row.

OPTIONS

Enjoy the slapstick additions of more recent years:

> Row, row, row your boat,
> Gently down the stream.
> If you see a crocodile,
> Don't forget to scream.

> Row, row, row your boat,
> Gently down the stream.
> Throw your teacher [*add any name here*] overboard
> And listen to them scream.

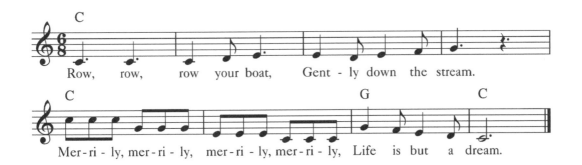

Row, row, row your boat,
Gently down the stream.
Merrily, merrily, merrily, merrily,
Life is but a dream.

Round and Round the Garden

IT'S ALWAYS felt ancient, this one, but it can't be that old since teddies were only established in 1903 (after an unsuccessful bear hunt by President Theodore 'Teddy' Roosevelt). It probably originated as a hare song:

Round about there,
Sat a little hare.
The bow wows came,
And chased him right up there!

The teddy version was collected around 1946.

I loved this one as a kid. I guess the idea of teddies dancing round gardens was always going to be a winner … and then there's the tickling. It has no melody as such. You can live dangerously and make up your own. And you can prolong the child's agony by pausing before speeding to the tickling zone.

ACTIONS

Grab someone's hand and turn it upwards. With one finger, draw circles round their palm as you sing, 'Round and round the garden, like a teddy bear', then take 'one step' up the arm with your middle finger, then 'two step' up the arm with your index finger, till you … 'a-tickly under there!' – and tickle under the arm.

Round and round the garden,
Like a teddy bear.
One step, two step,
And a-tickly under there!

Pat-a-Cake

THIS TRADITIONAL English song appeared in a 1698 comedy by a man called Thomas d'Urfey, where a 'tattling' nurse was heard murmuring the following: 'Ah Doddy blesse dat pitty face of myn Sylds, and his pitty, pitty hands, and his pitty, pitty foots, and all his pitty things, and pat a cake, pat a cake Bakers man, so I will master as I can, and prick it, and prick it, and prick it, and prick it, and throw't into the Oven.'

It's a good song for warming your hands on a cold day. Although if you were a sibling of mine, waiting for the school bus in Swansea in February 1981, you might have had to suffer the embarrassment of your mother taking the actions a little further and getting the whole bus queue to do jumping jacks, while shouting, 'This is the way we kept warm in Neath. Come on, everybody! Jump!'

On another, probably more interesting note, the idea of marking your bread with your initial/family mark came out of necessity. Communal ovens were common in the Middle Ages and more recent times, so it was useful to be able to recognize your food amongst the other cooked goods in there.

ACTIONS

Clap along, then prick the imaginary dough before throwing it in the air, I mean oven. *Or* clap with a partner. First clap your own hands together, then hit your right hand against your partner's right hand, then clap your own hands together again, then hit your partner's left hand with your left. Repeat.

OPTION

Use your child's initial instead of 'B' and their name instead of 'baby'.

Here's a variation:

> Patty cake, patty cake, baker's man,
> Bake me a cake as fast as you can.
> Roll it up, roll it up, and throw it in the pan!
> Patty cake, patty cake, baker's man.

There is also a similar song in Norwegian (see 'Bake kake søte', p. 156).

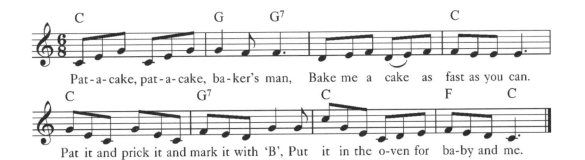

Pat-a-cake, pat-a-cake, baker's man,
Bake me a cake as fast as you can.
Pat it and prick it and mark it with 'B',
Put it in the oven for baby and me.

This Little Piggy

THIS SONG, or early versions of it, first appeared in print in the early 1700s. It is the most popular digit song of the last 150 years and has a very famous literary appearance to boot – it turns up in Dylan Thomas's play *Under Milk Wood* as part of jack of all trades Mister Waldo's dream.

But what is this obsession with feet? Is it because they become so ugly in later life even though they start off so lovely and soft?

My mother had another favourite song about feet. Let me take this opportunity to teach it to you. You'll never forget it. She has no idea where it comes from and a quick look for it online turns up articles on malaria, borax water, smelly socks and breast milk. Try it – I'm not lying. So the song, which again is a good one for improvising as there is no strict melody attached, goes like this: 'Put my head between your toes and smell your smelly feet, OH, Valencia!'

World-changing, this one.

And so to the more famous toe song (again, melody free).

ACTIONS

Start on any foot found in your vicinity (better clean than otherwise). I usually start with the big toe, grab it, and wriggle it and say out loud, 'This little piggy went to market', then move to the second largest toe, 'This little piggy stayed at home', and work down through the toes to the littlest one, 'And THIS little piggy' … and then keep them waiting …'went' … wait … 'WEEE' (random all-over-body tickling) 'WEEE, WEEE' – and end under the arms, 'All the way home.'

This little piggy went to market,
This little piggy stayed at home,
This little piggy ate roast beef,
And this little piggy had none,
And this little piggy went wee, wee, wee,
All the way home.

Incy Wincy Spider

THIS SONG first appeared in American publications in the early 1900s, and since then the spider has had more names than a royal baby, including 'Itsy Bitsy', 'Ipsy Wispy', 'Inky Binky' and 'Eency Weency'. Insert your favourite, but I learned it in this form.

ACTIONS

Touch your index finger to the thumb of your other hand, then (without taking that finger off) move your thumb up to the index finger of your second hand. Release the index finger of your first hand and rotate that hand (keeping its shape) so that the index finger is now uppermost, then move your second thumb up to that index finger (without taking the finger of that hand away from the thumb). Repeat the hand twisting to 'climb' up. Mimic rain falling with your hands and wash out the spider by sweeping your hands away from your body. Splay your hands open to mimic the sun's rays, then start digit climbing once more.

Incy Wincy spider
Climbed the water spout,
Down came the rain
And washed the spider out.
Out came the sun and
Dried up all the rain,
And Incy Wincy spider
Climbed up the spout again.

Baby Bumblebee

THIS IS A new one that we picked up in a small town called Greer, in a peach-growing area just outside Greenville, South Carolina. It appeared in Esther L. Nelson's *The World's Best Funny Songs* (1988).

ACTIONS

Clasp your hands together as if cupping a bumblebee, move your cupped hands to and fro to the rhythm; when you reach 'fuzzy wuzzy', vibrate them until 'OUCH!' when you open your hands wide as if you've been stung.

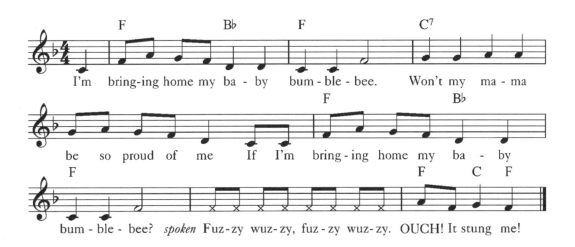

I'm bringing home my baby bumblebee.
Won't my mama be so proud of me
If I'm bringing home my baby bumblebee?
Fuzzy wuzzy, fuzzy wuzzy. OUCH! It stung me!

See Saw
Margery Daw

FIRST described in the early 1700s, this was probably sung by carpenters to keep a rhythm while using a two-handled saw. (Hence the 'penny a day' for slow work.) 'Margery' was a common name amongst the poor country folk of the eighteenth and nineteenth centuries. And from old meanings of 'daw', it may be deduced that 'Margery Daw' described a lady of loose morals. Which makes for a terrifying image in the first line. So let's set this aside for the moment, and move on to another unsavoury tale.

My six-year-old sister had dentures that I coveted. I'd often be found posing in front of the bathroom mirror with a double set of teeth while my sister hunted for them, all toothless and gummy. She'd lost her real teeth in 1972 on an iron horse somewhere near Sheffield. While singing this song she was 'bucked' out of her seat face first into the steel horse head.

ACTIONS

Sit on the floor, facing your partner, with your legs open wide and your feet touching your partner's. Hold hands, and pull and push back and forth ('seesaw') as you sing.

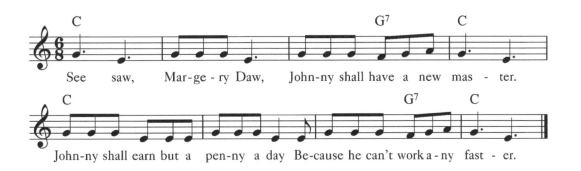

See saw, Mar-ge-ry Daw, John-ny shall have a new mas - ter.

John-ny shall earn but a pen-ny a day Be-cause he can't work a-ny fast - er.

See saw, Margery Daw,
Johnny shall have a new master.
Johnny shall earn but a penny a day
Because he can't work any faster.

Mynd ar y Ceffyl

YOU KNOW the ankle, that lovely jointed hook at the end of an adult's leg where you might sit (if still light enough) and gallop …? If you liked to do that as a child, well, this one's for you.

This is a traditional Welsh song. Read the phonetic version first, and don't worry about your accent. The Welsh accent varies so much from place to place that you can just fob off doubters with the 'This accent? It's my dialect' line.

ACTIONS

Sit child either on said ankle joint or, if your child is thriving too much and is just too heavy, sit them on your knees / lap, facing you or facing away. Basically, you are the horse, and you must move so as to give the child the impression they are having a whale of a time on their favourite palomino pony. Bump them up and down as you 'clippety clop' and 'trot, trot, trot', push them up high when you are going 'up to the mountain', lower them down when going 'to the dale', then bump them soundly on the 'far away' / 'boom, boom, boom' bit.

Mynd ar y ceffyl, clipi-di-clop,
Mynd ar y ceffyl, trot, trot, trot.
I lanc i'r mynydd, ach i lawr i'r cwm,
Draw dros y dolydd, bwm, bwm, bwm.

Gyrru a gyrru, gyrru a gyrru,
Gyrru a gyrru fel y gwynt. HO!

Repeat first verse

PHONETIC VERSION

Minn-d ar err keph-ill, clip a dee clop,
Minn-d ar err keph-ill, trot, trot, trot.
Ee lan ir mun-ith, ee la-oor ir comb,
Drow dross ur dol-eer, boom, boom, boom.

Gurry a-gurry, gurry a-gurry,
Gurry a-gurry, vel ur gwint. HO!

Here's an English version:
Ride on a pony, clippety clop,
Ride on a pony, trot, trot, trot.
Up to the mountain, down to the dale,
Over the hills and far away.

Gallop and gallop, gallop and gallop,
Gallop and gallop like the wind. HO!

Thumbelina

FROM THE 1952 film *Hans Christian Andersen*, this song was written by Frank Loesser (who also wrote the winter classic 'Baby, It's Cold Outside', which I recorded with Sir Tom Jones back in 1999). Loesser called the 'Thumbelina' song a 'ditty', saying, 'I could write that junk any day of the week.'

Incredible! I wish I could write such 'junk' so easily.

I had to include some Danny Kaye classics in this book; he's one of the best singalong actors that ever was. And as for Hans Christian Andersen – what a storyteller! 'The Steadfast Tin Soldier', 'The Little Mermaid', 'The Ugly Duckling' and 'The Little Match Girl' were all born of his imagination, and he published the story of tiny Thumbelina and her adventures in 1835.

ACTIONS

Your thumbs are now magical fairy creatures, dancing to the music as you sing.

['Wonderful Copenhagen', also written by Frank Loesser and performed by Danny Kaye, can be found on p. 114.]

So you're no bigger than my thumb, than my thumb, than my thumb;
Sweet Thumbelina, don't be glum.
Now, now, now, ah, ah, ah, come, come, come!

Thumbelina, Thumbelina, tiny little thing,
Thumbelina dance, Thumbelina sing.
Oh Thumbelina, what's the difference if you're very small?
When your heart is full of love, you're nine feet tall!

So you're no bigger than my toe, than my toe, than my toe,
Sweet Thumbelina, keep that glow;
And you'll grow, and you'll grow, and you'll grow.
Chorus

Humpty Dumpty

THE EARLIEST version of this song in print appeared in Samuel Arnold's *Juvenile Amusements* (1797). It became an international riddle, called 'Boule Boule' in France, 'Thille Lille' in Sweden, 'Trill Trolle' in Germany (and there are more). What falls off a wall and can't be put together again? An egg. But we all know the answer now, ever since Humpty was drawn as an egg in Lewis Carroll's *Through the Looking Glass* (1872).

Again, there are many interesting theories attached to this simple song. One claims it was the name of a cannon used in Charles I's fight against attacking Roundheads. The cannon fell down to the ground from a high position on the battlements and couldn't be fixed … 'Humpty dumpty' was an ale-and-brandy drink in the seventeenth century. It can also mean a short and/or clumsy person.

ACTIONS

This is a great one to amuse restless toddlers. Your knees are the wall and the toddler is Humpty – when you get to 'had a great fall' you lurch them over the edge (keeping a tight grip), bringing them back up again when you get to 'put Humpty together again'.

(A game which might predate the rhyme is one where girls sit down holding their skirts tightly around their feet. At a signal, they let themselves fall backwards and try to recover without letting go of the skirts.)

Humpty Dumpty sat on a wall,
Humpty Dumpty had a great fall.
All the king's horses and all the king's men
Couldn't put Humpty together again.

CHAPTER 2

If You're Happy and You Know it

'He who sings frightens away his ills'

~ MIGUEL DE CERVANTES, *DON QUIXOTE*

THERE IS A TENDENCY IN MUSICALS for the protagonists to just burst into song and/or dance when life is good. Well, this is that chapter. Life, even for a commuter in winter or a child stuck on the playground front line, will have its high moments, and on these days everything's just fine. There are always games aplenty to play when you are Mr Optimistic.

Reciting this old tongue twister, dating from the early 1800s, was thought to cure hiccups (say it through thrice without breathing) as well as helping singers and actors improve their diction. Step it up a notch by adding 'off a pewter plate' to each line.

> Peter Piper picked a peck of pickled peppers;
> A peck of pickled peppers Peter Piper picked.
> If Peter Piper picked a peck of pickled peppers,
> Where's the peck of pickled peppers Peter Piper picked?

There are also playground activities like kiss chase, clapping games, turning cartwheels (now criminally banned from schoolyards, on the grounds of health and safety), leapfrog and hopscotch. Or what about the tomato game? 'It' sits in the middle of a circle of people. Ask 'it' questions — they must answer 'tomato' to everything. 'How old are you?' 'Tomato.' 'What colour are your eyes?' 'Tomato.' And so on. Whoever makes 'it' laugh is next to take a turn in the middle.

Bear in mind, of course, that for those not currently sharing such good spirits, you will become the most annoying goofball on the planet. But whether you are high on life, love, strong coffee or sugar-buzz-tastic sherbet dip, nothing can deflate you at times like this and you need songs like the following to sing on your good ship *Happy*.

41

Zip-a-Dee-Doo-Dah

FROM DISNEY'S 1946 film *Song of the South*, this song was originally sung by James Baskett and written by Allie Wrubel and Ray Gilbert. It is, along with 'When You Wish Upon a Star' (see p. 236), an Academy Best Original Song Award-winner. The bluebird ('on my shoulder') has long been considered a symbol of cheer and contentment but they also serve a good purpose in the garden – they are voracious insect-eaters.

Zip-a-dee-doo-dah, zip-a-dee-ay,
My, oh my, what a wonderful day!
Plenty of sunshine headed my way,
Zip-a-dee-doo-dah, zip-a-dee-ay.

Mister bluebird's on my shoulder.
It's the truth,
It's actual,
Everything is satisfactual.

Zip-a-dee-doo-dah, zip-a-dee-ay,
Wonderful feeling, wonderful day!

Whistle While You Work

THIS SONG was written by Frank Churchill and Larry Morey for Disney's classic *Snow White and the Seven Dwarfs* (1937). The vocals in the film version are incredible – they are so high and remind me of Bollywood singers like Asha Bhosle. The singer (and the voice of Snow White) was actress Adriana Caselotti, whose older sister Louise gave Maria Callas vocal lessons, which always paints rather a curious picture.

Just whistle while you work [*whistle*]
And cheerfully together we can tidy up the place.
So hum a merry tune [*hum*]
It won't take long when there's a song to help you set the pace.

And as you sweep the room,
Imagine that the broom
Is someone that you love, and soon
You'll find you're dancing to the tune.

When hearts are high, the time will fly, so whistle while you work.

High Hopes

IN ANDALUSIA, in 2012, we'd watch ants walking in long rows up a table's legs and across the table top to find crumbs of bread, before making a U-turn, walking back across the table and down the legs to the hole in the wall, where they must have colonized. They'd be carrying crumbs at least ten times their size, and we began to imagine monster ants and what they might be able to achieve. A less relaxed ant incident occurred in the swamps of Louisiana in 2007, while I was filming a documentary on the Mississippi River. The director inadvertently stood on a nest of red imported fire ants. The result? Painfully blistered and tightly swollen lower limbs. There may be as many as 22,000 species of ant ... and they have been around for over 110 million years.

Here is the ultimate ant song, written by Jimmy Van Heusen and Sammy Cahn. It was used in the 1959 movie *A Hole in the Head* and popularized by Frank Sinatra.

Next time you're found, with your chin on the ground, There's a lot to be learned, so look a - round.___ Just what makes that lit-tle old ant_ Think he'll move that rub-ber tree plant? A-ny-one knows an ant can't Move a rub-ber tree plant. But he's got high___ hopes, he's got high___ hopes, He's got high, ap-ple - pie - in-the - sky___ hopes. So a - ny time you're get - tin' low, 'Stead of let - tin' go, Just re-mem-ber that ant. Oops, there goes a - no - ther rub - ber tree plant!

Next time you're found, with your chin on
   the ground,
There's a lot to be learned, so look around.

Just what makes that little old ant
Think he'll move that rubber tree plant?
Anyone knows an ant can't
Move a rubber tree plant.

But he's got high hopes, he's got high hopes,
He's got high, apple-pie-in-the-sky hopes.

So any time you're gettin' low,
'Stead of lettin' go,
Just remember that ant.
Oops, there goes another rubber tree plant!

The Tra La La Song

THE THEME for *The Banana Splits Adventure Hour* was written by Mark Barkan and Ritchie Adams and released in 1968 on Decca. The song hit the US charts that year, and a punk cover version made number 7 in the UK singles charts in 1979.

Saturday morning TV and its soundtracks loom large in this chapter – Saturday mornings in the 1970s must rank high in my good times chart. *Monkey*, reruns of old *Batman* shows, *The Banana Splits*, *The Monkees* … Growing up as one of four children, Saturday mornings were the crazy hours. Roly-polying in pyjamas, battling under upside-down armchairs and fighting over programme choice only added to the excitement. But this song was guaranteed to unite the enemies in a chorus of tra la las.

One banana, two banana, three banana, four,
Four bananas make a bunch and so do many more.
Over hill and highway the banana buggies go,
Comin' on to bring you the Banana Splits show.

Makin' up a mess of fun,
Makin' up a mess of fun,
Lots of fun for everyone.
Tra, la la, la la la la, tra la la, la la la la,
Tra la la, la la la la, tra la la, la la la la.

Four banana, three banana, two banana, one,
All bananas playin' in the bright warm sun.
Flippin' like a pancake, poppin' like a cork,
Fleegle, Bingo, Drooper an' Snork.
Chorus

The Bucket of Water Song

DO YOU REMEMBER the Four Bucketeers from the anarchic and utterly brilliant *Tiswas* – with The Cage and the Phantom Flan Flinger? I only recently found out that 'Tiswas' stood for 'Today Is Saturday, Watch and Smile'. Officially those Four Bucketeers were Chris Tarrant, Sally James, John Gorman and Bob Carolgees, with sporadic contribution from Lenny Henry. Written by John Gorman, the song was never intended as a lasting piece of musical magic, nor ever meant to be recorded. But it was, and it reached number 26 in the UK charts in 1980. And here it is, thirty and more years later …

*This is the song
We lovers of water sing.
We can't go wrong,
We're happy as a king.
We beat the drum as we march along,
We clash the cymbal and bang the gong.
We sing out strong,
The bucket of water song.*

Stand on one leg
And point up at the sun,
Breathe through your nose,
We're sure it must be fun.
No matter who or what you are,
We know something you'll enjoy by far –
To sing out this song,
The bucket of water song.
Chorus

[*Spoken*] Though life is hard,
We do the best we can.
Against evil we guard,
To help our fellow man.
We put the baddies in their place,
We fight the foes of the human race.
But whatever the case,
We take it in the face.

Repeat chorus three times, modulating up as you go.

Follow the Yellow Brick Road

IT'S HARD TO believe now that box-office returns were disappointing on the initial release of the gloriously Technicolor *Wizard of Oz* in 1939 – it has since become one of the best-loved films of all time. Judy Garland was always singing in our house when we were growing up; recordings, admittedly, but I imagined meeting her, watching her dance and sing, talk and laugh live. She was a mesmerizing performer whose absolute sacrifice to her craft/art is endlessly inspiring. I wrote the song 'Way Beyond Blue' (from our first album, of the same name) with Judy in mind, after reading her biography.

This song from the film was written by E. Y. Harburg and Harold Arlen.

Follow the Yellow Brick Road, follow the Yellow Brick Road,

Follow, follow, follow, follow, follow the Yellow Brick Road.

Follow the rainbow over the stream; follow the fellow who follows a dream.

Follow, follow, follow, follow, follow the Yellow Brick Road.

We're off to see the Wizard, the wonderful Wizard of Oz.

We hear he is a whizz of a Wiz if ever a whizz there was.

If ever, oh ever a whizz there was, the Wizard of Oz is one because,

Because, because, because, because, because,

Because of the wonderful things he does.

We're off to see the Wizard, the wonderful Wizard of Oz!

King of the Castle

THIS SONG is the oldest rhyme in the book, appearing in Horace's *Epistulae I* (*c.* 20 BC). Roman children would have sung it like this:

> *Rex erit qui recte faciet;*
> *Qui non faciet, non erit.*

Roughly translated this means: 'He will be king who acts well; anyone who doesn't, will not.'

Popular in 1700s Scotland was this version:

> Ian William of the Wastle,
> Am now in my Castle,
> And awe the Dogs in the Town
> Shan't gar me gang down.

ACTIONS

Find higher ground. A chair will do, or the top of a climbing frame. And claim it as your own by singing the song. Resist those who want your higher ground. Great for starting fights. Apparently, pulling at the 'king's clothes to get him down from his castle is strictly forbidden, under penalty of exclusion from the game … This rule never travelled over the River Severn to our house.

I'm the king of the castle,
Get down, you dirty rascal!

Ring a Ring o' Roses

SONGS sometimes get associated with historical events and their story becomes common currency, without it being based on any actual evidence. I've always been led to believe that this is a song about the Black Death of the 1340s or the Great Plague of 1665: The rosy rash? A symptom of the plague. The posies of herbs? To protect against infection, or to ward off the smell. The sneezing? What you did before you fell down dead. But though this theory is all good and 'rosy', it probably isn't true at all. It's been reported that a similar tune was evident in Massachusetts in 1790, but it was in 1881 that it first appeared in children's literature and it didn't have any 'atishoo's – the line was 'Hush, hush, hush'. But it is true that the song has travelled widely, presumably because children everywhere, of any era, love the drama of the last line, whether it be sitting, stooping, squatting, curtseying, bowing or just falling down.

Ring a ring o' roses,
A pocket full of posies.
Atishoo! Atishoo!
We all fall down.

Here We Go Round the Mulberry Bush

MULBERRIES don't, in fact, grow on bushes but rather on trees – similar songs exist in Scandinavia, but with a juniper tree. This is a traditional English song dating from the 1840s, and it's a happy song, but its origins may be a lot darker.

In the exercise yard of HMP Wakefield, the female inmates, along with their offspring, would walk around the mulberry tree growing there. Could the song have been born out of the need to entertain these children? And been sung while the inmates carried out their endless and mundane prison duties, as listed in the song? The association of mulberry trees with prisons began in the early nineteenth century when prisons started to get involved in silk production, as silkworms love mulberry leaves. Apparently, a mulberry tree still grows in the prison today.

ACTIONS

Dance around holding hands in a circle for the first verse, then break up to mimic the actions of each subsequent verse.

Here we go round the mul-berry bush, The mul-berry bush, the mul-berry bush.

Here we go round the mul-berry bush On a cold and frost - y morn - ing.

Here we go round the mulberry bush,
The mulberry bush, the mulberry bush.
Here we go round the mulberry bush
On a cold and frosty morning.

This is the way we wash our clothes ...
This is the way we dry our clothes ...
This is the way we iron our clothes ...
This is the way we mend our shoes ...
This is the way we bake our bread ...
This is the way we scrub [or 'sweep'] the floor ...
This is the way we go to church ...
This is the way the ladies walk ...
This is the way the gentlemen walk ...

In and Out the Dusty Bluebells

THIS IS ONE of those songs that echoes with the voices of children long gone. Though there is little evidence to prove its existence earlier than the mid twentieth century, some reports claim that it is older, originating in Ireland in the early 1900s, and possibly related to the hiring fairs in May (when Ireland is filled with bluebells). The children went to the fairs to get summer work from local farmers (hence 'You will be my master') – hard work with long, long hours and poor pay. But the song prevails as a happy one, and a very popular one, and there are some lovely old photos of children playing it in the streets. I can easily imagine those children in their three-quarter-length cotton dresses and huge leather boots, ringlets and ribbons, singing and dancing this song.

ACTIONS

Hold hands together in a large circle, with arms aloft, and walk so the circle turns. One child, the 'master', skips through the arches made by the arms, weaving in and out of the circle, then stops behind the child nearest her when the 'tippy, tappy' part is reached. She taps that child on their shoulder, then when 'You will be my master' is sung the picked child holds on to the 'master' and follows behind her as they proceed to skip through the arches. This is repeated until the children skipping in the chain behind the 'master' far outnumber the children in the circle. The game ends when only two children are left to form a last arch.

OPTIONS

You can use 'Scottish' or 'dusky bluebells' instead of 'dusty' ones, 'pit a pat' on shoulders instead of 'tippy, tappy', and/or 'partner' instead of 'master'.

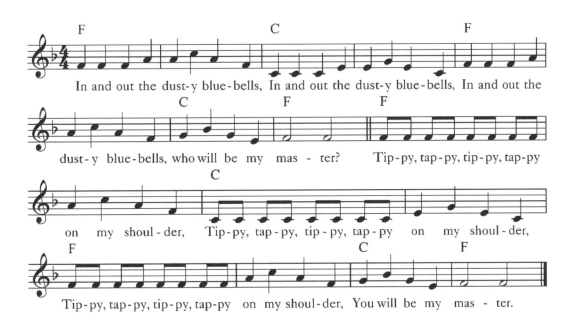

In and out the dusty bluebells,
In and out the dusty bluebells,
In and out the dusty bluebells,
Who will be my master?

Tippy, tappy, tippy, tappy on my shoulder,
Tippy, tappy, tippy, tappy on my shoulder,
Tippy, tappy, tippy, tappy on my shoulder,
You will be my master.

CHAPTER 3

Oh Dear, What Can the Matter Be?

*'Some days there won't be a song
in your heart. Sing anyway'*

~ EMORY AUSTIN

CHILDREN CAN BE MORBIDLY CURIOUS. Having a scientist and doctor as a father meant that at home, skeletons, pickled fingers and other assorted bits of anatomy in jars and medical encyclopaedias filled our shelves. Graphic and gory photographs of grisly murders and dissected prostates were pored over at night under the duvet. Our bunny rabbits were the frozen kind, ready for experimentation, and I'd play with the tendons of chicken feet (feet which I tried to grow once, in a souvenir jar from Scotland, till the smell of rotting flesh alerted others to my bedroom science). I got rather practical when it came to bloody or painful occurrences — any loose and wobbling tooth in a classmate's mouth could surely be removed with a swift twist of the wrist or a firm bump with a fist. Hence my nickname: The Dentist.

I also loved strange and frightening stories, like this one, 'The Tale of Nant Gwrtheyrn' (which is now a most beautiful venue for learning Welsh). An altar-bound bride plays a last game of hide and seek. She finds a hole in the trunk of an old tree and climbs into the dark. Nobody finds her, and she is trapped. And she waits. And waits. Many years later lightning strikes, breaking the old tree in two. Her skeleton is revealed, wisps of yellowed bridal lace blowing gently in the wind.

Children love to be scared, just a little, I suppose. Remember 'What's the Time, Mister Wolf?' or 'British Bulldogs', running absolutely petrified as the older, bigger children loomed behind you ready to smash soft flesh into concrete? Humans have long been fascinated by the unusual, and nursery rhymes and traditional songs were often used to inform and educate, and faced squarely up to subjects like death, ill health and misfortune — and I've always found them utterly compelling.

So welcome to our ghost train chapter. Enjoy the ride.

John Brown's Body

THIS SONG, from the mid nine-teenth century, is about the abolitionist John Brown, whose actions may have been instrumental in the outbreak of the American Civil War. It was popular with the Union soldiers and may have been written by one (or several) of them.

I loved to sing this as a child because it is so graphic yet hopeful, as the best is saved till last – in an afterlife in heaven. Julia Ward Howe was inspired to write 'The Battle Hymn of the Republic' after hearing troops sing this song.

John Brown's body lies a-rotting in the grave,
John Brown's body lies a-rotting in the grave,
John Brown's body lies a-rotting in the grave,
But his soul is marching on!

Glory, glory, hallelujah!
Glory, glory, hallelujah!
Glory, glory, hallelujah!
His soul is marching on!

He's gone to be a soldier in the army of the
    Lord, [×*3*]
But his soul is marching on!
Chorus

John Brown's knapsack is strapped upon his
    back, [×*3*]
But his soul is marching on!
Chorus

John Brown died that the slaves might be
    free, [×*3*]
But his soul is marching on!
Chorus

The stars above in Heaven now are looking
    kindly down, [×*3*]
But his soul is marching on!
Chorus

The House of the Rising Sun

THE TUNE of this American traditional song, about a house of ill repute, may have originated in England, with the lyrics added later in America. It's the first song I learned to play on guitar – many count it as their first tune too. (Learn that sweet Am chord and many songs will come easily.) Bob Dylan's version is still a favourite.

These are the traditional words, from the girl's perspective.

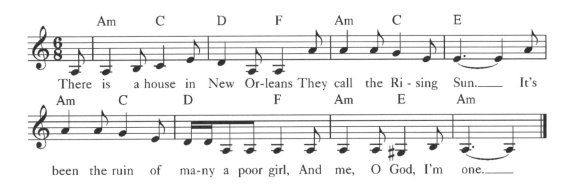

There is a house in New Orleans
They call the Rising Sun,
It's been the ruin of many a poor girl,
And me, O God, I'm one.

My mother was a tailor;
She sewed my new blue jeans.
My sweetheart was a gambler, Lord,
Down in New Orleans.

Now the only thing a gambler needs
Is a suitcase and a trunk,
And the only time he's satisfied
Is when he's on a drunk.

He fills his glasses up to the brim,
And he'll pass the cards around,
And the only pleasure he gets out of life
Is ramblin' from town to town.

Oh, tell my baby sister
Not to do what I have done,
But shun that house in New Orleans
They call the Rising Sun.

Well, it's one foot on the platform
And the other foot on the train,
I'm going back to New Orleans
To wear that ball and chain.

I'm a-going back to New Orleans,
My race is almost run.
I'm goin' back to end my life
Down in the Rising Sun.

There is a house in New Orleans
They call the Rising Sun,
It's been the ruin of many a poor girl,
And me, O God, I'm one.

St James Infirmary
Blues

THIS VERY American-sounding song, popularized by Louis Armstrong and Cab Calloway, and more recently Hugh Laurie, is thought to originate in England as a song called 'The Unfortunate Rake' – and St James was a hospital in London. The song, as songs can, evolved into another too, in this case 'Streets of Laredo'. I loved singing it as a very young child, though I didn't know how to pronounce 'pall bearers' for many years. It must have been funny to hear me sing the blues – in a child's voice and with a Swansea accent. I loved blues songs then, and I still do now.

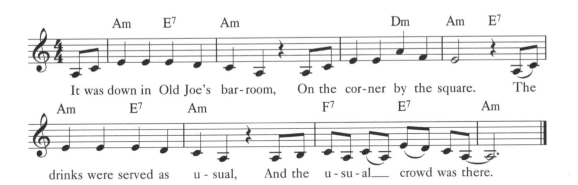

It was down in Old Joe's barroom,
On the corner by the square.
The drinks were served as usual,
And the usual crowd was there.

He was standing at my shoulder.
His eyes were bloodshot red.
He turned to the crowd around him;
These are the very words he said:

I went down to the St James Infirmary,
I saw my baby there.
She's laid out on a cold white table,
So *so* cold, so white, so fair.

Let her go, let her go, God bless her,
Wherever she may be.
She may search this wide world over,
She'll never find a sweet man like me.

Oh, when I die, bury me
In my high-top Stetson hat;
Put a twenty-dollar gold piece on my watch
   chain.
God'll know I died standin' pat.

I want six crap shooters for pall bearers,
Chorus girl to sing me a song.
Put a jazz band on my hearse wagon.
Raise Hell as I roll along.

Roll out your rubber-tired carriage,
Roll out your old-time hat.
Twelve men going to the graveyard,
And eleven coming back.

Now that I've told my story,
I'll take another shot of booze.
And if anyone should happen to ask you,
I've got those gamblers' blues.

Molly Malone

THIS IS a nineteenth-century Irish song, which, like 'Waltzing Matilda', has a ghostly ending. Fish was commonly sold in the streets, from three-wheeled carts often made of wicker.

There is a bronze statue of Molly in College Green, just off one end of Grafton Street. It seems the sculptor made the most of the legend that she was a professional in the oldest business in the world – her 'wares' being most obviously presented – and with true Dublin wit the statue has acquired alternative names: the 'tart with the cart', the 'trollop with the scallops', the 'dish with the fish'.

In Dublin's fair city, where the girls are so pretty,
I first set my eyes on sweet Molly Malone
As she wheeled her wheelbarrow, through streets broad and narrow,
Crying cockles and mussels, alive, alive-o!
Alive, alive-o! Alive, alive-o!
Crying cockles and mussels, alive, alive-o!

She was a fishmonger, but sure 'twas no wonder,
For so were her father and mother before,
And they each wheeled their barrow, through streets broad and narrow,
Chorus

She died of a fever, and no one could save her,
And that was the end of sweet Molly Malone.
But her ghost wheels her barrow, through streets broad and narrow,
Chorus

The Twa Brothers

THIS LOVELY, long story-led song is included in Child's ballad collection of the 1880s. It is a Scottish song – and one of my favourites. Scottish songs are often steeped in tragedy, blood and gore (while Welsh songs are often about yearning to be somewhere you are not).

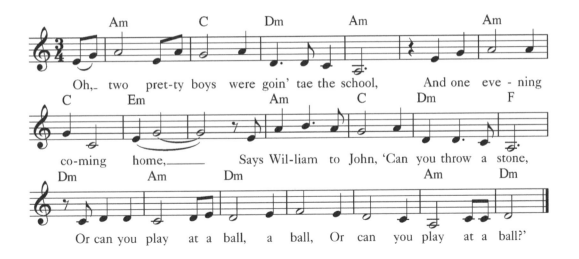

Oh,_ two pret-ty boys were goin' tae the school, And one eve - ning
co-ming home,_____ Says Wil-liam to John, 'Can you throw a stone,
Or can you play at a ball, a ball, Or can you play at a ball?'

Oh, two pretty boys were goin' tae the school,
And one evening coming home,
Says William to John, 'Can you throw a stone,
Or can you play at a ball, a ball,
Or can you play at a ball?'

Says John to William, 'I canna' throw a stone,
Little can I play at a ball.
But if you'll go down to yon merry green
    woods,
I'll try you a wrestlin' fall, a fall,
I'll try you a wrestlin' fall.'

So they wrestled up and they wrestled down
Beneath the spreadin' moon.
The little penknife stuck out of William's
    pocket
And gave John his deadly wound, wound,
And gave John his deadly wound.

'Ah, now you'll take off your white Holland
    shirt
And teer it frae gore tae gore,
And you will bind my deadly wounds
That they might bleed no more, no more,
That they might bleed no more.'

So he's ta'en off his white Holland shirt
And he's torn it frae gore tae gore,
And though he's bound his deadly wounds,
Ah, they bled ten times more, more,
They bled ten times more.

'Ah, but what shall I tell to your father dear,
This night when I go home?'
'Tell him I'm away to a London school
And a good scholar I'll come home, home,
A good scholar I'll come home.'

'Ah, but what shall I tell to your stepmother
    dear,
This night when I go home?'
'Tell her I'm dead and in the grave laid
For she prayed I might never come home,
    home,
She prayed I might never come home.'

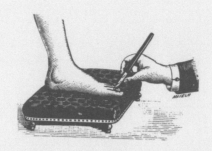

Who's Gonna Shoe Your Pretty Little Feet?

THIS ONE began life as the Scottish song 'Lass of Roch Royal' (Child Ballad 76, *c.* 1700), a song born out of class inequality, poverty and discrimination. It's sung by a mother, 'fair Annie', to her newborn baby, fathered by a lord (Lord Gregory) and born out of wedlock. Society cast out this single mother and, starving and cold, she went to knock on Lord Gregory's castle door ...

'O, open the door, Lord Gregory,
O, open, let me in,
For the wind blows through my
yellow hair
An' I'm shiverin' to the chin.'

His mother answered the door in the guise of her son.

'Awa', awa', ye vile woman,
Some evil deed may ye dae,

Ye're but some witch or vile
warlock
Or mermaid of the sea [...]
Now tell me some o' the love
tokens
That passed between you and me.'

Annie was sent away. Lord Gregory went looking for the girl and the baby the following day. He found them, both dead of starvation and exposure, on the shore near the castle. I love these old songs where, for a moment, you slip into the shoes of women living hundreds of years ago.

This desperately sad song migrated over to America with Scottish settlers, where it evolved into a love song, recorded by Woody Guthrie and Cisco Houston.

Who's gonna shoe your pretty little feet? Who's gonna glove your hand? Who's gonna kiss your red ruby lips? Who's gonna be your man?

Who's gonna shoe your pretty little feet?
Who's gonna glove your hand?
Who's gonna kiss your red ruby lips?
Who's gonna be your man?

Papa's gonna shoe my pretty little feet,
Momma's gonna glove my hand,
Sister's gonna kiss my red ruby lips,
I don't need no man.

I don't need no man,
I don't need no man,
Sister's gonna kiss my red ruby lips,
I don't need no man.

Fastest train I ever did ride
Was a hundred coaches long,
The only woman I ever did love
Was on that train and gone.

On that train and gone, boys,
On that train and gone,
Only woman I ever did love
Was on that train and gone.

Repeat first three verses

Grandma, Grandma

THIS IS one of my more recent finds. I learned it in 2011, when we moved my youngest to his London nursery. There are many versions worldwide and there is no melody as such – it's all about the rhythm. It sounds like it could have originally been a clapping or skipping song.

ACTIONS

Clap the rhythm really strongly, make the rhyme groove. Then follow the actions as you go.

Grandma, Grandma, sick in bed,
She sent for the doctor and the doctor said,
'Grandma, Grandma, you're not sick.
All you need is a walking stick!'

I said, hands up, shake, shake, shakety shake.
I said, hands down, shake, shake, shakety shake.
To the front uh-huh, to the back uh-huh,
To the s-s-side, to the s-s-side.

She never went to college,
She never went to school,
But I'd bet a bottom dollar
She could wriggle like a fool.

It's Raining, It's Pouring

MY MOTHER had three favourite songs that were not in her beloved Welsh language. One is 'Valencia' (see p. 26), and the next is this one (including a Welsh grammar corruption in line 6):

Knock on the door, [*knock on child's forehead*]
Peep in. [*lift an eyelid*]
Open the latch, [*lift the end of the nose*]
Walk in. [*open mouth*]
Take a chair, [*pinch a cheek*]
And sit by there. [*pinch the other cheek*]
How do you do, Mister Chinny-Chin-Chin? [*nod child's chin up and down*]

And the third is this traditional English rhyme (published in 1939). It's a mad one … Does the man die? Shouldn't he have gone to bed *after* bumping his head?

Conclusion? Some mothers like it odd.

It's raining, it's pouring,
The old man is snoring.
He went to bed and bumped his head,
And he couldn't get up in the morning.

London Bridge is Falling Down

WHEN I WAS a child my head was turned by old photographs found in songbooks and recipe books, rather than by posters of pop bands. It's so much easier to digest history when a melody or promise of food accompanies it. This is a fine example of a song that leads us to experience a little of a way of life that has long drifted down the river.

The first London Bridge was a wooden one built by the Romans around AD 55. It fell into disrepair when they left some 350 years later. The first stone bridge was built in the twelfth and thirteenth centuries; it was 60 feet high and 30 feet wide, complete with tower and gates. By the fourteenth century many people lived and traded on the bridge – some shops were three storeys high – but erosion by the current meant that costly repairs to the foundations were necessary. The people's worry that bridge repair money was being squandered may have manifested itself in this song. Though the earliest record of it dates from the mid 1700s, it may have originated in the Middle Ages.

London Bridge is falling down,
Falling down, falling down.
London Bridge is falling down,
My fair lady.

Build it up with wood and clay,
Wood and clay, wood and clay.
Build it up with wood and clay,
My fair lady.

Wood and clay will wash away ...

Build it up with bricks and mortar ...

Bricks and mortar will not stay ...

Build it up with iron and steel ...

Iron and steel will bend and bow ...

Build it up with silver and gold ...

Silver and gold will be stolen away ...

Set a man to watch all night ...

Suppose the man should fall asleep ... ?

Give him a pipe to smoke all night ...

Waltzing Matilda

THE FIRST ghost song of the book. It was written in 1895 by solicitor and poet A. B. 'Banjo' Paterson and his friend Christine Macpherson at Christine's farm, Dagworth Station, Queensland. The tune may be related to that of 'Thou Bonnie Woods of Craigielea'. Many Australians count this as their unofficial national anthem.

A 'swagman' is Australian slang for a tramp or a hobo who travels ('waltzes') around the country. Our swagman is sitting in the shade of a tree boiling up some water in a 'billy' (billycan) over a fire to make some tea, probably because he had no food for a meal. 'Matilda' is another slang word for 'swag' (i.e., the bundle of worldly possessions carried by the swagman tied up on the end of a stick). A 'billabong' is an oxbow lake, formed when a bend in a river is cut off as the river straightens out. A 'jumbuck' is a sheep. And a 'squatter' is an Australian landowner, representing authority and so not likely to be popular among former convicts. So the tramp, deciding he'd prefer to die than spend his life in jail for stealing 'tucker' (food), runs from the 'troopers' (cops) and kills himself by jumping into the billabong.

Once a jolly swagman camped by a
    billabong,
Under the shade of a coolibah tree.
He sang as he watched and waited 'til his
    billy boiled,
'You'll come a-waltzing, Matilda, with me.
Waltzing Matilda, Matilda, my darlin',
You'll come a-waltzing, Matilda, with me.'
He sang as he watched and waited 'til his
    billy boiled,
'You'll come a-waltzing, Matilda, with me.'

Well, down came a jumbuck to drink at
    the billabong;
Up jumped the swagman and grabbed him
    with glee.
He laughed as he stowed the jumbuck in
    his tucker-bag,
Chorus
He laughed as he stowed the jumbuck in
    his tucker-bag,
'You'll come a-waltzing, Matilda, with me.'

Well, up rode the squatter, mounted on his
    thoroughbred;
Up rode the troopers – one, two, three.
'Where's that jolly jumbuck you've got in
    your tucker-bag?
Chorus
Where's that jolly jumbuck you've got in
    your tucker-bag?
You'll come a-waltzing, Matilda, with me.'

Well, up jumped the swagman and jumped
    into the billabong;
'You'll never take me alive,' said he.
His ghost may be heard as you pass by the
    billabong:
Chorus
His ghost may be heard as you pass by the
    billabong:
'You'll come a-waltzing, Matilda, with me.'

And the Band Played 'Waltzing Matilda'

WRITTEN by Eric Bogle (a Scottish-born Australian singer-songwriter) in 1971, this is one of the most moving anti-war songs ever written.

When I was a young man I carried me pack
And I lived the free life of the rover;
From the Murray's green basin to the dusty
    outback
I waltzed my Matilda all over.
Then in 1915 my country said: 'Son,
It's time to stop rambling, there's work to be
    done.'
So they gave me a tin hat and they gave me
    a gun
And they sent me away to the war.

And the band played 'Waltzing Matilda'
As the ship pulled away from the quay,
And amidst all the tears, flag-waving and
    cheers
We sailed off for Gallipoli.

How well I remember that terrible day
When our blood stained the sand and the
    water
And how in that Hell they call Suvla Bay
We were butchered like lambs at the
    slaughter.
Johnny Turk, he was ready, he primed
    himself well.
He rained us with bullets, and he showered
    us with shell,
And in five minutes flat we were all blown
    to Hell.
He nearly blew us back home to Australia.

And the band played 'Waltzing Matilda'
When we stopped to bury our slain.
Well, we buried ours and the Turks buried
    theirs,
Then it started all over again.

Oh, those that were living just tried to
    survive
In that mad world of blood, death and fire,
And for ten weary weeks I kept myself alive
While around me the corpses piled higher.
Then a big Turkish shell knocked me arse
    over head,
And when I awoke in me hospital bed
And saw what it had done, I wished I was
    dead.
I never knew there was worse things than
    dying.

Oh, no more I'll go waltzing Matilda
All around the green bush far and near,
For to hump tent and pegs, a man needs
    both legs.
No more waltzing Matilda for me.

They collected the wounded, the crippled,
    the maimed
And they shipped us back home to
    Australia,
The armless, the legless, the blind and the
    insane,
Those proud wounded heroes of Suvla.
And when the ship pulled into Circular
    Quay
I looked at the place where me legs used to
    be
And thank Christ there was no one there
    waiting for me
To grieve and to mourn and to pity.

And the Band played 'Waltzing Matilda'
When they carried us down the gangway.
Oh, nobody cheered, they just stood there
    and stared,
Then they turned all their faces away.

Now every April I sit on my porch
And I watch the parade pass before me.
I see my old comrades, how proudly they
    march
Renewing their dreams of past glories.
I see the old men all tired, stiff and worn,
Those weary old heroes of a forgotten war,
And the young people ask 'What are they
    marching for?'
And I ask myself the same question.

And the band plays 'Waltzing Matilda'
And the old men still answer the call.
But year after year, their numbers get fewer –
Someday no one will march there at all.

Waltzing Matilda, waltzing Matilda,
Who'll come a-waltzing Matilda with me?
And their ghosts may be heard as they
    march by the billabong,
So who'll come a-waltzing Matilda with me?

CHAPTER 4

Nana's Tune Emporium

*'Sweetest the strain when in the song
The singer has been lost'*

~ ELIZABETH STUART PHELPS WARD

I WAS GOING TO HAVE an 'Oh no, not again!' chapter, including such titles as 'Kumbaya', 'Morning Has Broken', 'Ging Gang Goolie', 'I Know a Song That Gets on Everybody's Nerves' (repeat infinitely and you've got it), 'Ten Green Bottles' (counting songs seem to prolong the agony as you are well aware of how long you've to go till it ends), 'The Twelve Days of Christmas', etc., etc. — all those songs give me an all-too-real flashback to horrible, damp, imaginary (I never did camp with Scouts) Scouting moments: bursting for the toilet in the freezing cold, breathing tent air while outside the dark clouds hover and the rain is horizontal, sitting round a non-firing fire with all-too-enthusiastically singing campers ...

But the beauty of music is that it's subjective — you may feel all warm and mushy when reminded of these songs, and even want to sing them. I'm afraid you'll have to look them up elsewhere. So, if you don't mind, I'll introduce you now to my new idea.

These were my nana's favourites. I found many in the piano stool she gave me when I was seven, me being so keen on playing her piano. When the world seemed impenetrably confusing, my punchbag piano was the best relief. One song from the stool that I'm not including here is 'Oh, for the Wings, for the Wings of a Dove', which is a great one to ruin – and I did, often, so let's leave it in peace for now.

I love to play these old tunes next to brand-new releases on my radio show. Many of their lyrics predate political correctness and serve to underline today's shiny blandness. But I'll spare you the more fruity hokum, for now anyway.

All together now ...

Doing the Lambeth Walk

CHECK OUT *Lambeth Walk – Nazi Style*, a re-edited film of goosestepping Nazi soldiers made by the British Ministry of Information in 1942 to boost morale. Hitler was said to be absolutely infuriated by it.

ACTIONS

Take eight steps forward, turn arm in arm with your partner, facing in one direction for four, then turn for four, then take eight steps forward again. Turn in a circle, alone this time, for four, slap your thighs three times, then on the fourth beat shout 'OY!' while bending your elbows with fists in the air. And repeat.

Lam-beth you've ne-ver seen, The skies ain't blue, the grass ain't green. It has-n't got the

May-fair touch, But that don't mat-ter ve-ry much. We play the Lam-beth way,

Not like you but a bit more gay, And when we have a bit of fun, Oh, boy!___

A - ny time you're Lam-beth way,__ A - ny eve - ning, a - ny day,__
Ev - 'ry lit - tle Lam-beth gal__ With her lit - tle Lam-beth pal,__

You'll find us all do-in' the Lam-beth walk. walk. Oy!
You'll find 'em all do-in' the Lam-beth

Ev-'ry-thing's free and ea - sy, Do as you darn well plea- sey,

Why don't you make your way there, Go there, stay there?

Lambeth you've never seen,
The skies ain't blue, the grass ain't green.
It hasn't got the Mayfair touch,
But that don't matter very much.
We play the Lambeth way,
Not like you but a bit more gay,
And when we have a bit of fun,
Oh, boy!

Any time you're Lambeth way,
Any evening, any day,
You'll find us all doin' the Lambeth walk.
Ev'ry little Lambeth gal
With her little Lambeth pal,
You'll find 'em all doin' the Lambeth walk.
OY!

Ev'rything's free and easy,
Do as you darn well pleasey,
Why don't you make your way there,
Go there, stay there?

Any time you're Lambeth way,
Any evening, any day,
You'll find us all doin' the Lambeth walk.
Ev'ry little Lambeth gal
With her little Lambeth pal,
You'll find 'em all doin' the Lambeth walk.
OY!

Yes! We Have No Bananas

WRITTEN BY Frank Silver and Irving Cohn for 1922's *Make It Snappy* Broadway revue, it's absolutely addictive, this song, usually sung in a terrible Greek accent (like 'Speedy Gonzalez', it was written before cultural/racial stereotyping in songs became unacceptable). It is quite shocking to hear it with today's ears, but I love it none the less, as it conjures up the great spirit of the hardworking fruit-seller and the positive message is sublime.

There's a fruit store on our street,
It's run by a Greek,
And he keeps good things to eat
But you should hear him speak!
When you ask him anything,
He never answers 'no',
He just 'yes'es you to death,
And as he takes your dough
He tells you,
'Yes, we have no bananas,
We have-a no bananas today.
We've string beans, and onions,
Cabashes, and scallions,
And all sorts of fruit and, say,
We have an old-fashioned tomato,
A Long Island potato.
But yes, we have no bananas,
We have no bananas today.'

Business got so good for him
That he wrote home to say,
'Send me Pete and Nick and Jim;
I need help right away.'
When he got them in the store,
There was fun, you bet.
Someone asked for 'sparrow grass'
And then the whole quartet
All answered,
'Yes, we have no bananas,
We have-a no bananas today.
Just try those coconuts,
Those wall-nuts and doughnuts.
There ain't many nuts like they.
We'll sell you two kinds of red herring,
Dark brown, and ball-bearing,
But yes, we have no bananas,
We have no bananas today.'

Pack Up Your Troubles in Your Old Kit-Bag

WRITTEN by George Henry Powell (under the pseudonym George Asaf) and set to music by his brother Felix, this song was published in 1915.

It was used as a marching song in the First World War and enjoyed worldwide popularity – there are versions in Dutch and Spanish. The title of Wilfred Owen's bitter anti-war poem 'Smile, Smile, Smile' (September 1918) came from this song.

Pack up your trou-bles in your old kit-bag, And smile, smile, smile,
While you've a Lu-ci-fer to light your fag, Smile, boys, that's the style.
What's the use of wor-ry-ing? It ne-ver was worth-while, so
Pack up your trou-bles in your old kit-bag, And smile, smile, smile.

Pack up your troubles in your old kit-bag,
And smile, smile, smile.
While you've a Lucifer to light your fag,
Smile, boys, that's the style.
What's the use of worrying?
It never was worthwhile, so
Pack up your troubles in your old kit-bag,
And smile, smile, smile.'

Private Perks is a funny little codger,
With a smile, a funny smile.
Five feet none, he's an artful little dodger,
With a smile, a funny smile.
Flush or broke, he'll have his little joke,
He can't be suppress'd.
All the other fellows have to grin
When he gets this off his chest. 'Hi!

Private Perks went a-marching into Flanders,
With his smile, his funny smile.
He was lov'd by the privates and
    commanders
For his smile, his funny smile.
When a throng of Bosches came along
With a mighty swing,
Perks yell'd out, 'This little bunch is mine!
Keep your heads down, boys and sing. Hi!
Chorus × 2

Private Perks he came back from Bosche-
    shooting,
With his smile his funny smile.
Round his home he then set about recruiting,
With his smile his funny smile.
He told all his pals, the short, the tall,
What a time he'd had;
And as each enlisted like a man,
Private Perks said, 'Now, my lad. Hi!
Chorus × 2

It's a Long Way to Tipperary

IRISHMAN Jack Judge apparently wrote this for a five-shilling bet in 1912, though it's also co-credited to Henry James Williams. It's a 'partner song' to 'Pack Up Your Troubles …', so try splitting into two groups, one singing one song while the other group sings the other.

OPTION

This extra verse (which I love) was popular with young soldiers marching to war. Doesn't this imply we didn't French kiss before?

> That's the wrong way to tickle Mary,
> That's the wrong way to kiss!
> Don't you know that over here, lad,
> They like it best like this!
> Hooray *pour les Françaises*!
> Farewell, *Angleterre*!
> We didn't know the way to tickle Mary,
> But we learned how, over there!

Up to mighty London came
An Irish lad one day,
All the streets were paved with gold,
So everyone was gay!
Singing songs of Piccadilly,
Strand, and Leicester Square,
'Til Paddy got excited and
He shouted to them there:

It's a long way to Tipperary,
It's a long way to go.
It's a long way to Tipperary
To the sweetest girl I know!
Goodbye Piccadilly,
Farewell Leicester Square!
It's a long long way to Tipperary,
But my heart's right there.

My Old Man Said Follow the Van

THIS SONG, written in 1919 by Fred W. Leigh and Charles Collins, is great for practising your Cockney accent, wherever you're from. But the humour belies the underlying story of the deprivation that working-class people were facing. A couple have to leave their home with all their possessions because they can't afford to pay their rent. There is no room for the wife in the van, so she follows on foot with her pet bird. Typically in the music-hall tradition, the song deals with these hardships in a determinedly upbeat fashion.

K-K-K-Katy

I'VE ONLY JUST discovered this ditty on vinyl at the back of a dusty old record store and I love it. My other half (being a whopping ten years older than me and having heard it way more times) is a little less enthusiastic ... It was a popular First World War song, written by Geoffrey O'Hara in 1917. The sheet music (published in 1918) advertised it as 'The Sensational Stammering Song Success Sung by the Soldiers and Sailors'. It has the most infectious and addictive chorus and (I warn you) is guaranteed to stay in your head for weeks.

Jimmy was a soldier brave and bold,
Katy was a maid with hair of gold,
Like an act of fate,
Kate was standing at the gate,
Watching all the boys on dress parade.
Jimmy with the girls was just a gawk,
Stuttered ev'ry time he tried to talk.
Still that night at eight,
He was there at Katy's gate,
Stuttering to her this love sick cry.

K-K-K-Katy, beautiful Katy,
You're the only g-g-g-girl that I adore;
When the m-m-m-moon shines,
Over the cowshed,
I'll be waiting at the k-k-k-kitchen door.
[Repeat]

No one ever looked so nice and neat,
No one could be just as cute and sweet,
That's what Jimmy thought
When the wedding ring he bought.
Now he's off to France the foe to meet.
Jimmy thought he'd like to take a chance,
See if he could make the Kaiser dance,
Stepping to a tune,
All about the silv'ry moon,
This is what they hear in far-off France.
Chorus

The Runaway Train

DAD = a buff corduroy (thick rows) hat with a greasy tidemark inside, a black driving jacket, shiny and thin with age, billows of blue Clan tobacco smoke from his pipe, and always the faint smell of Indian spices and lime pickle. Three things were true during the late 70s: we always ate curries; I always sat behind Dad on car journeys, clouds of Clan in my face; and I was always the one who was motion sick. This one is for him – he would sing it in the car. I associate it with elephants; I guess because Nellie the Elephant ran away too.

The song was written by Robert E. Massey, with music by Harry Warren and Carson Robison. Vernon Dalhart, whose real name was Marion Try Slaughter, released a version in 1931.

'Twas in the year of '89, on that old Chicago
line
When the winter wind was blowin' shrill,
The rails were froze, the wheels were cold,
then the air brakes wouldn't hold,
And Number Nine came roaring down the
hill – oh!

The runaway train came down the track
and she blew,
The runaway train came down the track
and she blew,
The runaway train came down the track,
her whistle wide and her throttle back,
And she blew, blew, blew, blew, blew.

The fireman said he rang the bell and she
blew,
The fireman said he rang the bell and she
blew,
The fireman said he rang the bell – the
engineer said, 'You did like hell!'
And she blew, blew, blew, blew, blew.

A donkey was standing in the way and she
blew,
A donkey was standing in the way and she
blew,
A donkey was standing in the way and all
they found was just his bray,
And she blew, blew, blew, blew, blew.

Show Me the Way to Go Home

THIS English folk song was adapted in 1925 by the songwriting team known together as Irving King. It reminds me of my favourite winter's evening … Rich smells of yeast, malt and old tights full of hops (nice) hung heavy in our house. A clothes-boiling machine, full of home-brew, sent yeast bubbles foaming all over the floor. It was an old Pembrokeshire recipe – and for clear heads a recipe for disaster. No fewer than three adults and a just-about-old-enough-to-drink youth were carried vomiting to bed that night. We ran out of buckets. Mum said she felt like a twisted Florence Nightingale but I was content to have a bad story I could bribe good people with in the cold light of day. The clothes-boiler stayed in the garage, empty and quiet, after that.

OPTIONS

There are other verses made up of synonyms of the first.

One version reads:

Indicate the way to my abode,
I'm fatigued and I want to retire.
I had a spot of beverage sixty minutes ago
And it went right to my cerebellum.

Wherever I may perambulate,
On land, or sea or atmospheric vapour,
You can always hear me crooning the melody
Indicate the way to my abode.

And another:

Lead me to my bed,
I'm knackered and I want to get some kip.
I had a bit of booze about an hour ago,
And it went right to my cop.

Wherever I may stroll,
To the pub, or to the dole,
You will always hear me making this noise,
Lead me to my bed.

Show me the way to go home,
I'm tired and I want to go to bed.
I had a little drink about an hour ago
And it's gone straight to my head.

Wherever I may roam,
On land or sea or foam,
You will always hear me singing this song,
Show me the way to go home.

Pop Goes the Weasel

I ALWAYS thought this song was about a weasel-fur purse 'popping' open, but apparently it's not. 'Weasel and stoat' means 'coat' in Cockney rhyming slang, and 'popping the weasel' means pawning the coat, perhaps after a big night at the Eagle pub. The 'monkey' in the song may refer to a glazed jug or tankard full of grog, as this is what a Victorian sailor would have called it, and 'knocking off a stick' meant to drink alcohol. The area of London referred to (now-fashionable Hoxton, Shoreditch and Spitalfields) was full of textile-industry sweatshops – but also full of places for the entertainment of the workers. A pub called the Eagle is still found at the corner of Shepherdess Walk and City Road, though it's not the original building. It's interesting to note that a 'spinners' weasel' was a mechanical device used to measure out a length of thread. It popped to indicate when the right length had been reached.

In the 1850s the song travelled to America as a dance craze, and plenty more verses were added.

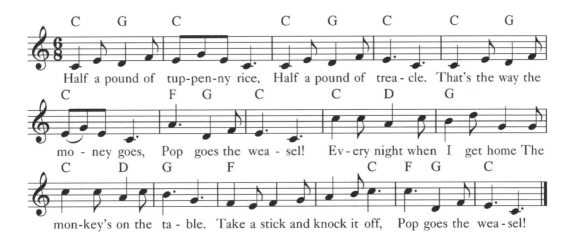

Half a pound of tuppenny rice,
Half a pound of treacle.
That's the way the money goes,
Pop goes the weasel!

Every night when I get home
The monkey's on the table.
Take a stick and knock it off,
Pop goes the weasel!

Up and down the City Road,
In and out the Eagle,
That's the way the money goes,
Pop goes the weasel!

I Like Bananas Because They Have No Bones

THIS SONG, written by Chris Yachich, appeared on compilations of novelty songs between 1914 and 1945; the version I know best was recorded by the Hoosier Hot Shots in 1935. When I played this recently on my radio show, it delighted a younger listener. He had thought his grandfather, who used to sing it about the house, had made it up.

For this one, all the words are included in the music, in the easy key of C.

CHAPTER 5

Let's Go Fly a Kite

*'Sing out loud in the car even, or especially,
if it embarrasses your children'*

~ MARILYN PENLAND

NOSTALGIA KICKS IN WITH FULL FORCE with this chapter. Summers in my memory were endless, with sun-filled, yawning, lazy, hay-baled, lust-filled, barn-swinging holidays … The reality? Rain, rain, rain on a tin caravan roof, kerosene fires, bunkbed fights (two beds, four children), smelly wellies, shivering cold, periwinkles on a pin, a bucket of mackerel in blood-pink water, fighting over never enough freshly-fried-in-a-saucepan chips, hail drumming louder on the tin roof, sand everywhere but on the beach, slurry and silage smells. Whenever we could, we'd head over to West Wales for some rest and recuperation — but none for Mum, with no washing machine in the rainy nation.

I grew up in the 70s and 80s, just as the popular package holidays of the straw donkey and cornrow hair kicked in, and on rare (though very welcome) occasions we would head not west but south, down to the hot sun, but not by plane. We'd travel in our battered car, foil in the window, eating canned ravioli and singing our way through the 35°-plus midsummer South of France. Dad didn't like stopping, so no water, no toilets. Just more 'Speedy Gonzalez' on repeat. Here's to that jar of summer goodness.

Let's Go Fly a Kite

THIS SONG was written by Robert B. Sherman for the 1964 Disney film *Mary Poppins*, starring Julie Andrews and Dick Van Dyke.

Recently we went to Dunstable Downs, which, despite telltale signs of the times – electronic gadgets, smart phones, the aeroplanes dragging gliders into the skies, and music playing for gatherings of all sorts of folk – somehow transcended time, as if it had, in essence, hardly changed over centuries. It's a perfect place to fly kites – which we did. (It is also a Site of Special Scientific Interest (SSSI), designated for the quality of its chalk grasslands. And it has two Scheduled Ancient Monuments, Five Knolls and Medieval Rabbit Warrens, and plenty of other historical features to make a visit totally worthwhile, not just for singing this song.)

With tuppence for paper and strings,
You can have your own set of wings.
With your feet on the ground,
You're a bird in flight,
With your fist holding tight
To the string of your kite!

Let's go fly a kite
Up to the highest height!
Let's go fly a kite
And send it soaring
Up through the atmosphere,
Up where the air is clear.
Oh, let's go fly a kite!

When you send it flying up there,
All at once you're lighter than air!
You can dance on the breeze,
Over 'ouses and trees,
With your fist 'olding tight
To the string of your kite!
Chorus

Istanbul
(Not Constantinople)

WRITTEN BY Jimmy Kennedy and Nat Simon, and first released by The Four Lads in 1953, this song smashes into being with the full force of its Middle Eastern string intro, then runs straight on with a stream of exotic-sounding place names. It got me from the get-go, and I'd sing 'People just like it better that way' as low as a high-pitched eight-year-old voice could manage.

It still sounds fresh and unhinged. I like songs that way.

Istanbul was Constantinople,
Now it's Istanbul, not Constantinople,
Been a long time gone, Old Constantinople
Still has Turkish delight
On a moonlit night.

Every gal in Constantinople
Is a Miss-stanbul, not Constantinople,
So if you've a date in Constantinople,
She'll be waiting in Istanbul.

Even old New York was once New
   Amsterdam,
Why they changed it, I can't say
(People just liked it better that way).

Take me back to Constantinople.
No, you can't go back to Constantinople,
Now it's Istanbul, not Constantinople.
Why did Constantinople get the works?
That's nobody's business but the Turks'.

Istanbul! Istanbul! 'Stanbul!

Wonderful Copenhagen

RED ROOFS, yellow roofs, blue roofs and green roofs, fir trees, lakes, hills, black shadows, then more red roofs, yellow roofs, blue roofs … This was the ticker-tape view from the window of the back lounge of our bus one night during our tour of Scandinavia. I couldn't sleep after a show and was the only one awake, bar the driver, and I spent the small hours just dreaming as the countryside flew by. Copenhagen was a destination on that tour, and this song takes me right back to that most idyllic, quiet, black night.

It's another song written by Frank Loesser and sung by Danny Kaye in the 1952 film *Hans Christian Andersen* (see 'Thumbelina', p. 36), and it is now the official song of the city of Copenhagen.

Wonderful, wonderful Copenhagen,
Friendly old girl of a town
'Neath her tavern light
On this merry night
Let us clink and drink one down
To wonderful, wonderful Copenhagen
Salty old queen of the sea.
Once I sailed away
But I'm home today
Singing Copenhagen, wonderful, wonderful
Copenhagen for me

I sailed up the Skagerrak
And sailed down the Kattegat
Through the harbor and up to the quay
And there she stands waiting for me
With a welcome so warm and so gay.
Chorus

Summer Holiday

WRITTEN BY Peter Myers and Ronald Cass for the film of the same name, this song (as well as three others from the film's soundtrack) went to the top of the chart in 1963. The film, a smash hit at the box office, starred a very young and dashing Cliff Richard, and the large cast also included Una Stubbs and The Shadows. Herbert Ross's choreography was breathtaking. I blame this film for my still-burning ambition to drive through Europe in a transit van, with guitar and mattress all in.

We're all going on a summer holiday,
No more working for a week or two.
Fun and laughter on our summer holiday,
No more worries for me or you,
For a week or two.

We're going where the sun shines brightly,
We're going where the sea is blue.
We've all seen it on the movies,
Now let's see if it's true.

Everybody has a summer holiday,
Doin' things they always wanted to,
So we're going on a summer holiday,
To make our dreams come true,
For me and you,
For me and you.

Speedy Gonzalez

SO HERE it is – that song. Picture us, in the mid 1970s driving through France in August, four probably chickenpoxed children broiling on the back seat. We travelled with a plastic box full of badly recorded 'pop' music, numbered in marker pen over drug-company cassettes (all you had to do was tape over the holes and record over the promotional spiel). Other songs on these cassettes were Sonny and Cher's 'I Got You, Babe', 'Bobby's Girl', 'Que Sera Sera', 'Have I the Right to Hold You?', 'The Ugly Bug Ball' and 'Seven Little Girls Sitting in the Back Seat'.

But it was this song which prevailed as no. 1 with the back-seaters, written in 1961, by Buddy Kaye, Ethel Lee and David Hess. Pat Boone's version was a worldwide million-selling hit single in 1962.

[*Spoken*] It was a moonlit night in Old
  Mexico.
I walked alone between some old adobe
  haciendas.
Suddenly, I heard the plaintive cry of a
  young Mexican girl:

La la la, la la la la la la la la la,
la la la la la la la la la, la la la la la la la la.

You better come home Speedy Gonzales,
    away from Tannery Row.
Stop all of your drinking with that floosie
    named Flo!
Come on home to your adobe and slap some
    mud on the wall!
The roof is leaking like a strainer. There's
    loads of roaches in the hall.
(*La la la la*)

Mmm, Speedy Gonzales (Speedy
    Gonzales),
Why don't you come home?
Speedy Gonzales (Speedy Gonzales),
How come you leave me all alone?

[*spoken*] 'Hey Rosita, I have to go shopping
downtown for my mother – she needs some
tortillas and chilli peppers!'

Your doggie's gonna have a puppy, and we're
    running out of Coke.
No enchiladas in the icebox, and the
    television's broke.
I saw some lipstick on your sweatshirt, I
    smell some perfume in your ear.
Well, if you're gonna keep on messin', don't
    bring your business back a-here.
(*La la la la*)

Kookaburra

THIS SONG was the subject of a copyright wrangle – spot its melody in the Men At Work hit 'Down Under'. It was written in 1932 by Australian teacher Marion Sinclair. She entered the song into a Girl Guide competition, which it won. This is a good one for singing in a round.

We toured extensively in Australia in the late 90s. It would always tickle us to arrive in a city thousands of miles away, often after nearly two days of travelling, to perform in a venue almost exclusively filled to the rafters with Welsh expats. At one particularly memorable gig in Melbourne, the Super Furry Animals arrived, adding another huge dollop of the red, white and green.

Koo-ka-bur-ra sits in the old gum tree.   Mer-ry, mer-ry king of the bush is   he.

Laugh,   Koo-ka-bur- ra! Laugh,   Koo-ka-bur- ra! Gay your life must   be.

Kookaburra sits in the old gum tree.
Merry, merry king of the bush is he.
Laugh, Kookaburra! Laugh, Kookaburra!
Gay your life must be.

Kookaburra sits in the old gum tree
Eating all the gum drops he can see.
Stop, Kookaburra! Stop, Kookaburra!
Leave some there for me.

Kookaburra sits in the old gum tree
Counting all the monkeys he can see.
Stop, Kookaburra! Stop, Kookaburra!
That's not a monkey that's me.

Kookaburra sits on a rusty nail,
Gets a boo-boo in his tail.
Cry, Kookaburra! Cry, Kookaburra!
Oh, how life can be.

A Windmill in Old Amsterdam

WRITTEN BY Myles Rudge (who also wrote 'Hole in the Ground' and 'Right Said Fred'), this song was a million-selling record for 50s crooner Ronnie Hilton in 1965, just before his career stalled under the wheels of a newcomer – rock 'n' roll. It gives a child the idea that Amsterdam is all mice, cheese, clogs, tulips and windmills. When we first played the Paradiso, it was with some whimsical regret that we found Amsterdam a very modern, albeit handsome, city.

A mouse lived in a windmill in old
    Amsterdam,
A windmill with a mouse in and he wasn't
    grousin'.
He sang every morning, 'How lucky I am,
Living in a windmill in old Amsterdam!'

I saw a mouse!
Where?
There on the stair!
Where on the stair?
Right there!
A little mouse with clogs on.
Well, I declare!
Going clip-clippety-clop on the stair.
Oh yeah.

This mouse he got lonesome, he took him
    a wife.
A windmill with mice in, it's hardly
    surprisin'.
She sang every morning, 'How lucky I am,
Living in a windmill in old Amsterdam!'
Chorus

First they had triplets and then they had
    quins.
A windmill with quins in, and triplets and
    twins in.
They sang every morning, 'How lucky we
    are,
Living in a windmill in Amsterdam, ya!'
Chorus

A mouse lived in a windmill, so snug and so
    nice.
There's nobody there now but a whole lot
    of mice!

Eviva España

THIS IS the 70s equivalent of Rihanna's 'Birthday Cake' (the remix version). Though not as suggestive as that contemporary pop song, it still oozes waywardness through and through.

When you look at the lyrics it really is quite silly, but the associations are deeply ingrained … maybe it's those holiday memories of acres of sizzling skin and sweet sangria, and the start of turbulent teenage hormones?

You can now sing this song in more than ten languages. It was written by Belgian writers Leo Caerts and Leo Rozenstraten and originally released in 1971. Its popularity in the 70s coincided perfectly with the explosion of affordable Spanish package holidays. Sylvia had a massive hit with it in English in 1974. Check out her appearance on *Top of the Pops* with obligatory straw hat.

The ladies fell for Rudolph Valentino,
He had a beano back in those balmy days.
He knew every time you meet an icy creature,
You got to teach her hot-blooded Latin ways.
But even Rudy would have felt the strain
Of making smooth advances in the rain.

Oh, this year I'm off to sunny Spain. Eviva
España!
I'm taking the Costa Brava plane. Eviva España!
*If you'd like to chat a matador, in some cool
cabaña,*
And meet señoritas by the score, España, por
favour!

When they first arrive, the girls are pink and
pasty,
But, oh, so tasty, as soon as they grow brown.
I guess they know every fella will be queueing
To do the wooing his girlfriend won't allow.
But still I think today's a lucky day,
That's why I've learned the way to shout '*Olé!*'
Chorus

The Wee Article

THIS IS a traditional Irish song. I've enjoyed singing it ever since I learned to play the guitar. I always wonder why it's not more popular – the female protagonist is so feisty, especially considering her humble background.

I'm a jolly servant lass, my name is Mary Ann,
I'm going to sing about a thing that calls itself a man;
He wanted me his wife to be, he's only four foot four,
And this is how I answered him when talking at the door.

Ah, go wa', you daft wee article, you're nothing but a sham,
Common sense is anything that constitutes a man;
You're not the size of tuppence and your income isn't thruppence,
You may find a lass to love you, but it won't be Mary Ann.

To see this little article, with laughter you'd explode:
His legs is like the letter K and his eyes look every road,
But still he has the impudence to want a lass like me –
An article that you'd require a microscope to see.
Chorus

If we went walking down the street I'd have him at command,
For I could take him up like suds and blow him off my hand;
He says he'd buy me dresses and treat me like a queen,
He cannot treat himself, poor man; such a sight you've never seen!

Polly, Put the Kettle On

THIS SONG comes from a poem by Thomas Dale called 'Molly, Put the Kettle On', published in 1809. The tune may be related to that of the Viennese folk song 'O du Lieber Augustin' (1788), about a street musician who fell into a plague-ridden pit (he survived). The selection of songs you grow up with depends on where you were and the choices of your parents. I'm not so familiar with this one and keep melding it with 'London Bridge Is Falling Down'. Still, I rather like it, as it is clearly a call for tea and crumpets.

OPTIONS

Alternative last lines: 'It will all boil away' or 'We'll have no more today'.

('Polly' was a pet form of Mary, and 'Sukey' of Susan, in the middle-class mid eighteenth century.)

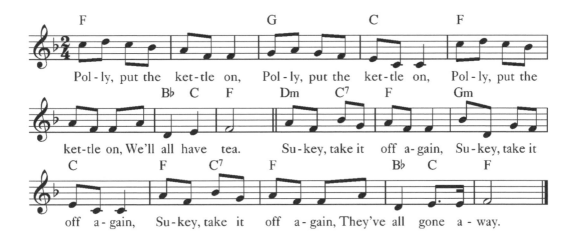

Polly, put the kettle on,
Polly, put the kettle on,
Polly, put the kettle on,
We'll all have tea.

Sukey, take it off again,
Sukey, take it off again,
Sukey, take it off again,
They've all gone away.

Blow the fire and make some toast,
Put the muffins down to roast,
Blow the fire and make some toast,
We'll all have tea.

Under the Bramble Bushes

MY SISTER and I, if we weren't being made to sing Woody Guthrie's 'This Land Is Your Land' in close harmony on repeat, were generally to be found in the woods behind our house in Swansea, running in a pack with the other local children. I loved these woods, full of rubbish and discarded top-shelf magazines (true), both despite and because of their strange fruit. I loved the exploration, the discovery and, of course, the plants. I would eat wild rhubarb, munching on the soft new shoots, which grew so fast, and picking at the bamboo-like older dry and reedy stems. The smell that hit you right away was wild garlic, with its dark-green, shiny cold leaves and little white flowers. Sometimes we'd sit under a fallen tree looking at the different types of fungus, wondering at their questionable names (like the blood-red, flat and fleshy 'Jew's ear'). Rhiannon was called Nannw Nannw (as in *Mork and Mindy*).

My sister and I would occasionally sing this clapping song, starting slow, then getting faster and faster until we were clapping as furiously as we could.

Under the bramble bushes, down by the sea,
    boom, boom, boom,
True love for you my darling, true love for me.
And when we marry, we'll raise a family,
With a boy for you and a girl for me,
And that's the way it's going to be, oh!

Repeat until you've had enough.

CHAPTER 6

Monoglots to Polyglots

'The clearest way into the Universe
is through a forest wilderness'

~ JOHN MUIR

REGARDING THE TOWER OF BABEL, why would God, on seeing all mankind coexisting, cooperating, talking one language and with the potential to achieve great things, see this as so wrong? But it did *not* please him and so he threw the proverbial spanner in the works by striking down the heaven-reaching architectural marvel and creating havoc by making mankind talk in hundreds of different languages.

I love languages. I was brought up bilingual and then later started learning French. French exchanges spent as a sulky teenager forced to watch *Inspecteur Gadget* (I loathe most cartoons) left me relatively fluent and at eighteen I left home for Spain, with the heaviest rucksack on my back filled with too many shoes (soon ditched) and a guitar. I was off to learn how to master the flamenco *rasgueado* technique. I recently returned to Seville and got the exact same reaction as before: incredulous hilarity, followed by disgust and then by the taking away of the guitar to be put back into a Spaniard's hands. You can't get by in music without a thick skin. Still, it's a pride-bruiser. I guess this goes some way to explaining why I never did master the *rasgueado* despite living in Spain for a year. I can, however, cook a mean paella, speak Spanish and some Catalan, and avoid water bombs thrown by children from upper-floor windows (don't ask).

Recent linguistic challenges include Mandarin and Japanese and annoying people at the Guča trumpet festival by repeatedly counting to ten in a Slavic brogue while partying hard on *rakia* (beware the *rakia*).

Now, a great way to kill a song is to sing it in an unfamiliar language. This is your chance. Murder on your lounge floor. You can 'cuckoo' in German, 'prick' in Norwegian, mime in French, ride goats in Irish.

Au Clair de la Lune

THIS eighteenth-century French song is great for learning a basic scale, and also has the honour of being the tune recorded by Édouard-Léon Scott de Martinville on 9 April 1860, which remains the earliest clearly recognizable recording of the human voice. It's worth checking his recording out – he also sings scales which are rather out of tune.

TRANSLATION

'By the light of the moon, my friend Pierrot, please lend me your pen, so I can write a note. My candle is out and I haven't a light; open the door, for the love of God.' By the light of the moon, Pierrot replies, "I don't have a pen and am now in my bed. Go see the neighbour; I think that she's in, because in her kitchen a lighter was sparked." By the light of the moon, likeable Lubin knocks on the brunette's door. She at once responds, "Who's that knocking so?" And he says in reply, "Open the door, for the God of Love!" By the light of the moon, one could barely see; they looked for the pen, they looked for a light. Searching like that, who knows what they found, but I do know this, they'd closed the door sound!'

Don't you think this song implies there's a little loving going on behind that door?

Au clair de la lune,
Mon ami Pierrot,
Prête-moi ta plume
Pour écrire un mot.
Ma chandelle est morte,
Je n'ai plus de feu.
Ouvre-moi ta porte,
Pour l'amour de Dieu!

Au clair de la lune,
Pierrot répondit:
'Je n'ai pas de plume,
Je suis dans mon lit.
Va chez la voisine,
Je crois qu'elle y est,
Car dans sa cuisine
On bat le briquet.'

Au clair de la lune,
L'aimable Lubin
Frappe chez la brune.
Elle répond soudain:
'Qui frappe de la sorte?'
Il dit à son tour:
'Ouvrez votre porte,
Pour le Dieu d'Amour.'

Au clair de la lune,
On n'y voit qu'un peu.
On chercha la plume,
On chercha le feu.
En cherchant d'la sorte,
Je n'sais c'qu'on trouva;
Mais je sais qu'la porte
Sur eux se ferma.

Alouette

THIS traditional French folk song is a cruel one, not that I don't enjoy game, but the singer's intention is cunningly hidden behind a loving voice. 'Gentle lark' … Oh, the sweet-voiced hunter! With love he attracts, with gun he shoots! Singing this song, you become a sweet-voiced butcher: 'I gently PLUCK YOUR FEATHERS OFF YOUR HEAD, YOUR BEAK, YOUR NECK, YOUR BACK, YOUR TAIL …' until there's nothing left but the edible meat. Nothing gentle about the fate of this bird. Nevertheless it's extremely popular, sung all over the world in many different languages.

TRANSLATION

'Lark, gentle lark, Lark, I'm going to pluck you, I'm going to pluck your beak … eyes … head … neck … back … wings … belly … legs … tail.'

A - lou-et - te, gen - tille a-lou-et - te, A - lou-et - te, je te plu-me-rai.
Je te plu-me-rai le bec, Je te plu-me-rai le bec, Et le bec, et le bec.
A - lou-ette, A - lou-ette! Ah! Ah! Ah! Ah! A - lou - et - te,
gen - tille a - lou - et - te, A - lou-et - te, je te plu-me-rai.

Alouette, gentille alouette,
Alouette, je te plumerai.
Je te plumerai le bec,
Je te plumerai le bec,
Et le bec, et le bec.
Alouette, Alouette!
Ah! Ah! Ah! Ah!
Alouette, gentille alouette,
Alouette, je te plumerai.

Alouette, gentille alouette,
Alouette, je te plumerai.
Je te plumerai les yeux,
Je te plumerai les yeux,
Et les yeux, et les yeux,
Et le bec, et le bec.
Alouette, Alouette!
Ah! Ah! Ah! Ah!
Alouette, gentille alouette,
Alouette, je te plumerai.

Alouette, gentille alouette,
Alouette, je te plumerai.
Je te plumerai la tête ...

Je te plumerai le cou ...

Je te plumerai le dos ...

Je te plumerai les ailes ...

Je te plumerai le ventre ...

Je te plumerai les pattes ...

Je te plumerai la queue ...

Sur le pont d'Avignon

THIS French folk song dates back to the fifteenth century. Originally one would have sung '*sous*' – dancing under (rather than 'on', '*sur*') the bridge, where it crossed the Île de Barthelasse, was the custom in medieval times.

ACTIONS

Pairs of dancers, arm in arm and facing in opposite directions, circle on one spot. When you get to each verse do right by the character described: bow as the handsome gentlemen, curtsey as the beautiful ladies, march and salute as the soldiers, and play an air instrument of your choice as the musicians. At the end of each verse, join up with your partner and turn arm in arm on the spot again. *Or* you may all walk towards a centre point, raising your arms as you do so – 'Ho!' – then fall back into pairs and turn.

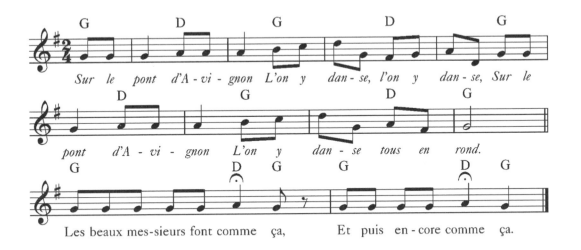

Sur le pont d'Avignon
L'on y danse, l'on y danse,
Sur le pont d'Avignon
L'on y danse tous en rond.

Les beaux messieurs font comme ça,
Et puis encore comme ça.
Chorus

Les belles dames font comme ça,
Et puis encore comme ça.
Chorus

Les militaries font comme ça ...
Chorus

Les musiciens font comme ça ...
Chorus

Frère Jacques

THE MELODY of this old French nursery song dates from the 1700s, with possible links to Italian and Hungarian tunes. It's completely entrenched in Chinese culture too, as it's the tune of an extremely popular children's song.

It's also a similar tune to that of 'Three Blind Mice', so they can be sung together in canon forms.

TRANSLATION

'Are you sleeping, are you sleeping, Brother John? Brother John? Ring the bells for morning prayers! Ring the bells for morning prayers! Ding, dang, dong. Ding, dang, dong.'

Frère Jacques, frère Jacques,
Dormez vous? Dormez vous?
Sonnez les matines! Sonnez les matines!
Din, dan, don. Din, dan, don.

Un Canard a Dit

THIS SONG will stick with you for ever once you've learned it. It's a favourite (of mine, not necessarily of the children) to sing in the car at top volume. I learned it from a Belgian American girl in Greenville, South Carolina.

It's a cunning play on words in French since '*ris, cane*' sounds the same as '*ricane*', which means 'to giggle', and '*la cane a ri*' sounds like '*le canary*' ('the canary'). I always imagine too a cannery where they fill cans with foie gras – no laughing matter.

TRANSLATION

'A drake said to his female duck, "Laugh, duck, laugh, duck." A drake said to his female duck, "Laugh, duck," and the duck laughed.

Un canard a dit a sa cane,
'Ris, cane, ris, cane.'
Un canard a dit a sa cane,
'Ris, cane,' et la cane a ri.

Fhir a' bháta

POPULAR IN Irish and Scottish Gaelic, this song was written in the late 1800s by Sìne NicFhionnlaigh from the Lewis village of Tong, inspired by her love of a fisherman ('The Boatman' of the title). They married soon after the song was written.

It takes me right back to an idyllic few weeks spent in the Outer Hebrides, some 20 years ago now, wandering through the flower-filled tracts of land, dotted by long-haired Red Angus cows and the odd tiny grass-roofed croft. Those empty stretches of white sands and clear turquoise seas are hard to beat, but then I was invited on to a schooner to shuck scallops and clean crabs with the crew. Nothing more romantic than cleaning crabs on those sticky wooden ship decks.

TRANSLATION

Boatman, boatman, sna oro ey-la, boatman, boatman, sna oro ey-la, boatman, boatman, sna oro ey-la, I wish you well wherever you roam! I climb the highest hill to try and catch sight of my boatman. Will he come today? Tomorrow? How sad I'll be if he does not. My broken heart aches and my eyes overflow with tears. Will you come tonight? I'll be waiting, or will I sigh and sadly close the door? I often ask the other boatmen, have they seen you? Are you OK? Every one of them replies that I'm a fool to give my love to you.

Fhir a' bhàta, 's na ho ro eile,
Fhir a' bhàta, 's na ho ro eile,
Fhir a' bhàta, 's na ho ro eile,
Mo shoraidh slàn leat 's gach àit' an tèid thu.

'S tric mi sealltinn o'n chnoc a's àirde,
Feuch am faic mi fear a' bhàta,
An tig thu an-diugh, no'n tig thu a-màireach,
'S mur tig thu idir gur truagh a tha mi.

Chorus

Tha mo chridhe-sa briste, brùite
'S tric na deòir a' ruith o'm shùilean.
An tig thu a-nochd, no am bi mo dhùil riut,
No'n dùin mi'n dorus le osna thùrsaich?

Chorus

'S tric mi foighneachd de luchd nam bàta
Am faic iad thu, no am bheil thu sàbhailt'?
Ach 's ann a tha gach aon dhiubh 'g ràitinn
Gur gòrach mise, ma thug mi gràdh dhuit.

Chorus

An Poc ar buile

GALE-FORCE WINDS were the welcome we expected in Gweedore, Donegal, but there was so much more: snow-capped Mount Errigal, soda bread, chips, more chips, pints of the black stuff and music. Everywhere. Frankie Kennedy's music school is held over the New Year and our children went along to one of the day's activities. This was the song they learned to sing (while parading under a giant paper fish).

The song itself ('The Mad Billy Goat') celebrates the story behind Puck Fair, held every August in Killorglin, in County Kerry, a festival which dates back to the seventeenth century. The story goes that a herd of wild mountain goats were disturbed by Oliver Cromwell's men. They scattered into the hills – except for one, who ran into Killorglin down below, giving the villagers warning that the army was coming. They took cover and survived, and have commemorated the event with the fair every year since.

TRANSLATION

As I set out with my stick in my hand to Dromore Town to join the neighbourhood work gang, I met a brown puck goat in fine roaring mad form. *Ailliliú, puilliliú, ailliliú*, it's the mad puck goat! *Ailliliú, puilliliú, ailliliú*, it's the mad puck goat! He chased me over the bramble and bush and over and through the bogland, 'til he caught his horns in a clump of gorse and without fear I jumped on his back. He ran through all the rocks with as much force as would destroy me, then he made the most almighty leap to the big slope of Faille Brice. Then the sergeant stood in Rochestown with his guards to apprehend us. The goat tore the man's trousers down – his breeches and new suspenders were left in rags. In Dingle Town the following afternoon, the parish priest addressed a meeting. He swore he'd seen the Devil himself riding on a mad puck goat!

Ag gabháil dom sior chun Droichead Uí
    Mhóradha
Píce im dhóid 's mé ag dul i meithil
Cé casfaí orm i gcuma ceoidh
Ach pocán crón is é ar buile.

*Ailliliú, puilliliú, ailliliú tá an poc
ar buile!*
Ailliliú, puilliliú, ailliliú tá an poc ar buile!

Do ritheamar trasna trí ruillógach,
Is do ghluais an comhrac ar fud na muinge,
Is treascairt do bhfuair sé sna turtóga
Chuas ina ainneoin ina dhrom le fuinneamh.
Chorus

Níor fhág sé carraig go raibh scót ann
Ná gur rith le fórsa chun mé a mhilleadh,
S'Ansan sea do cháith sé an léim ba mhó.
Le fána mhór na Faille Bríce.
Chorus

Bhí garda mór i mBaile an Róistigh
Is bhailigh fórsa chun sinn a chlipeadh
Do bhuail sé rop dá adhairc sa tóin ann
S'dá bhríste nua do dhein sé giobail.
Chorus

I nDaingean Uí Chúis le haghaidh an
    tráthnóna
Bhí an sagart paróiste amach 'nár gcoinnibh
Is é dúirt gurbh é an diabhal ba Dhóigh leis
A ghaibh an treo ar phocán buile.

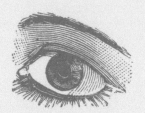

Cielito lindo

Written in 1882 by Mexican Quirino Mendoza Cortes, this is a great song and perfect for this stage of the book: 'SING! DON'T CRY!' It's a popular tune for mariachi bands to play while supporting their sports teams.

TRANSLATION

From the Sierra Morena, heavenly one, come a pair of sultry black eyes that steal a glance. Ay, ay, ay, ay! Sing, don't cry, because, those who sing, heavenly girl, gladden hearts. That beauty spot, heavenly one, by your mouth, Give it to nobody, it's for my touch alone.

De la Sierra Morena,
Cielito lindo, vienen
bajando,
Un par de ojitos negros,
Cielito lindo, de
contrabando.
Chorus

Ay, ay, ay, ay!
Canta, no llores,
Porque cantando se alegran,
Cielito lindo, los corazones.

Ese lunar que tienes,
Cielito lindo, junto a la boca,
No se lo des a nadie,
Cielito lindo, que a mi me
toca.
Chorus

Auf einem Baum
ein Kuckuck

THAT THE cuckoo in this song had the good fortune of a second coming of sorts reminds me of my own near death experience. It happened one hot, sweaty day on the small republic of Nauru, a very interesting place formally known as Pleasant Island. Not so pleasant that day when, due to an unplanned layover and the ever-present humidity, I decided to take a dip. Big mistake. Not even Michael Phelps could have coped with those tropical island currents (I hadn't yet heard the 'never swim' advice given to visitors).

I was dragged out into that vast Pacific Ocean quicker than you could say phosphate. More by luck than judgement I felt for sand below me and just about got hold with a big toe. Saved, within an inch of my life. My toe, that is. I edged slowly back to shore, half swimming, half creeping and totally terrified. But back to the cuckoo song, which first appeared in print in 1838. Try adding your own random cuckoo noises, and think back to the days of yore when the coming of the cuckoo meant the onset of better weather and more secret trysts with your lover.

TRANSLATION

'There's a cuckoo in a tree, Simsaladim, sits a cuckoo. There passed a young hunter, there passed a young hunter, a young hunter boy. He shot the poor cuckoo he shot the poor cuckoo, he shot him and he died, and when a year had gone by, and when a year had gone by. The cuckoo returned, the cuckoo returned. And the people rejoiced, and the people rejoiced.'

Auf einem Baum ein Kuckuck
Simsaladim, bamba, saladu, saladim
Auf einem Baum ein Kuckuck sass.

Da kam ein junger Jägers-
Simsaladim, bamba, saladu, saladim
Da kam ein junger Jägersmann.

Der schoss den armen Kuckuck
Simsaladim, bamba, saladu, saladim
Der schoss den armen Kuckuck tot.

Und als ein Jahr vergangen
Simsaladim, bamba, saladu, saladim
Und als ein Jahr vergangen war.

Da war der Kuckuck wieder
Simsaladim, bamba, saladu, saladim
Da war der Kuckuck wieder da.

Da freuten sich die Leute
Simsaladim, bamba, saladu, saladim
Da freuten sich die Leute sehr.

Three-Cornered Hat

THE MOST popular subjects make the most universal songs. Here is a fine example. Generations of people seemed to be very fond of this design of hat, from the 1600s on. No wonder: they were more than just a head cover, they were a fashionable gutter system and directed rainwater away from the shoulders.

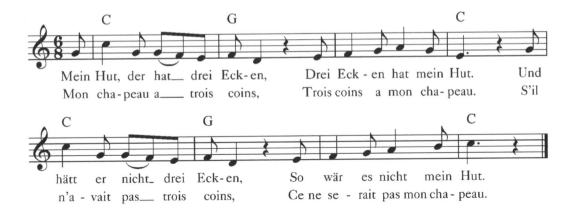

Mein Hut, der hat— drei Eck-en,   Drei Eck-en hat mein Hut.   Und
Mon cha-peau a— trois coins,   Trois coins a mon cha-peau.   S'il

hätt er nicht— drei Eck-en,   So wär es nicht mein Hut.
n'a-vait pas— trois coins,   Ce ne se-rait pas mon cha-peau.

[*German*] Mein Hut, der hat drei Ecken,
Drei Ecken hat mein Hut.
Und hätt er nicht drei Ecken,
So wär es nicht mein Hut.

[*French*] Mon chapeau a trois coins,
Trois coins a mon chapeau.
S'il n'avait pas trois coins,
Ce ne serait pas mon chapeau.

[*English*] My hat has three corners,
Three corners has my hat.
Had it not three corners,
It wouldn't be my hat.

[*Welsh*] Mae gen i het trichornel,
Tri chornel sydd i'm het.
Ac os nad oes tri chornel,
Nid honno yw fy het.

[*Hebrew*] תוניפ שולש ילש עבוכל
ילש עבוכל תוניפ שולש
תוניפ שולש ול ויה אל םא
ילש עבוכה הז היה אל

Idzie rak

THIS POLISH rhyme's a tickling game: walk your fingers from the child's tummy to tickle under the arms.

The Polish word for a crawling baby is '*raczkuja*'.

TRANSLATION

A crayfish comes, poor thing. But when it pinches, It'll leave its mark!

PHONETICS

Ee jeh rack
knee uir bo rack
iack oosh-tea pea knee-ay
Ben jeh znack

Idzie rak,
Nieborak.
Jak uszczypníe,
Będzie znak.

Bake kake søte

THIS IS a Norwegian clapping song for children. There are many versions.

ACTIONS

Clap along till the old man comes, then pretend to prick holes in your cake (which is in one of your hands) with said gold stick.

TRANSLATION

'Bake a sweet cake, dip it in cream, first in the cream, then in the water. Along comes an old man who will prick the cake with his small gold stick. Prick, prick, prick.'

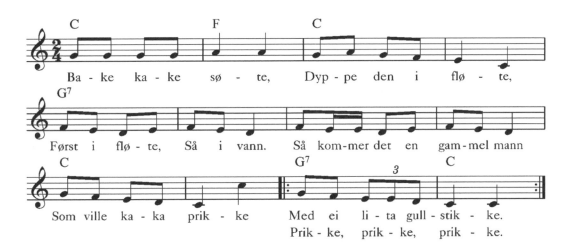

Bake kake søte,

Dyppe den i fløte,

Først i fløte,

Så i vann.

Så kommer det en gammel mann

Som ville kaka prikke

Med ei lita gullstikke.

Prikke, prikke, prikke.

Mochyn du

HERE'S A traditional folk song from early-eighteenth-century West Wales. '*Mochyn du*' means 'black pig'. Keeping pigs was common in rural Wales – they provided valuable sustenance through the long winter months and ate household scraps. Somehow it now reminds me of the story I read recently which explained the name of a savoury fried doughnut/dumpling that they serve commonly in the Southern United States: the hushpuppy. Apparently, during the Great Depression, people would throw these starchy balls to their hungry and whining dogs, calling out, 'Hush, puppies, hush, puppies!' In this song, overfeeding kills the pig.

OPTION

There are many versions of this song. Another favourite verse is roughly translated as follows:

The black pig has died.
Mum and Dad are crying.
They buried him in the orchard
With his nose sticking out.

TRANSLATION

'All you hill and county dwellers, come listen to this story, about an old pig who suddenly died. (Oh, how mournful we are, how heavy our hearts, after burying the black pig!) What caused his ailments? What killed him? Was it fresh whey that caused him to suddenly "go home"? Mum and Dad are crying their eyes out; the black pig is dead, and they dug an excellent grave for him in Carncoediog. Go get a hearse from Cardigan, and some horses to pull it, to show respect for the pig. Look up to the hooks, they are empty. There's not one iota to give any man – losing that pig was a great loss. Now I'm ending, putting the singing away, and urging you not to follow this bad example when you feed your pig.'

Holl drigolion bro a bryniau,
Dewch i wrando hyn o eiriau,
Fe gewch hanes rhyw hen fochyn
A fu farw yn dra sydyn.

O mor drwm yr ydym ni,
O mor drwm yr ydym ni,
Y mae yma alar calon
Ar ol claddu`r mochyn du.

Beth oedd achos ei afiechyd?
Beth roes derfyn ar ei fywyd?
Ai maidd glas oedd achos ange
I`r hen fochyn i fynd adre?
Chorus

Dad a mam yn crio`n arw,
Mochyn du sy wedi marw
Ac fe weithiwyd bedd ardderchog
I`r hen fochyn yn Carncoediog.
Chorus

Mofyn hers o Aberteifi
A cheffylau i`w thynnu fyny,
Y ceffylau yn llawn mwrnin
Er mwyn dangos parch i`r mochyn.
Chorus

Edrych fyny ar y bachau
Gweld hwy`n wag heb yr ystlysau
Dim un tamaid i roi undyn
Colled fawr oedd colli`r fochyn
Chorus

Ballach rydwyf yn terfynu
Nawr, gan roddi heibio canu
Gan ddymuno peidiwch dilyn
Siampl ddrwg wrth fwydo`r mochyn.
Chorus

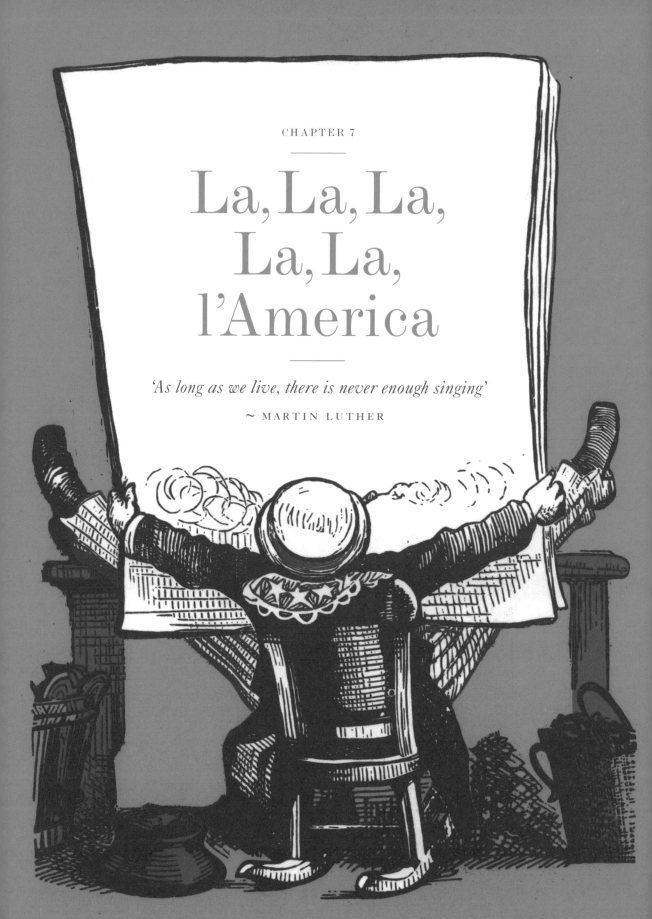

CHAPTER 7

La, La, La, La, La, l'America

'As long as we live, there is never enough singing'

~ MARTIN LUTHER

A LOVE–HATE RELATIONSHIP is what I have with America. But I return twice every year, to collect music on road trips. I do not enjoy America's coffee, butter substitutes, news channels, newspapers, plastic disposable cutlery and plates; but I can't get enough of its music.

Strangely enough, I got fascinated by the place through singing Irish tunes as a child, from a fabulous collection (*Soodlum's Irish Ballad Book*, 1981). I recognized parts of their melodies or themes and lyrics in other collections I enjoyed, like the music in Harry Smith's *Anthology of American Folk Music* (1927–40) and the work of folk singers like Bob Dylan, Woody Guthrie and Lead Belly. I loved the idea that songs travel way further and remain alive far longer than we can, and I became intrigued by American folk, where European folk came head to head with the music and rhythms sung and played by African slaves. With these old songs, it's not just the melody and rhythms, nor the sound of the words, that pulls me in, but rather the secrets they reveal, the social history they contain. In 2000 I decided to follow the journey of those Old World songs to the New World, where I settled a while. You will find mention of some well-travelled songs in this chapter.

Oh! Susanna

THIS SONG was written by Stephen Foster, a bookkeeper by trade, and first published in 1848. Due to copyright complications, he received only $100 for the song, despite its popularity amongst the minstrel troupes of the day. Eventually a publisher went some way to improve the situation.

I come from Alabama
With my banjo on my knee;
I'm going to Louisiana
My true love for to see.
It rained all night the day I left,
The weather it was dry;
The sun so hot I froze to death –
Susanna, don't you cry.

Oh! Susanna,
Oh, don't you cry for me,
For I come from Alabama
With my banjo on my knee.

I had a dream the other night,
When everything was still;
I thought I saw Susanna
A-coming down the hill.
The buckwheat cake was in her mouth,
The tear was in her eye.
Says I, I'm coming from the south,
Susanna, don't you cry.
Chorus

Home on the Range

FIRST published in 1873, the original poem was written by Dr Brewster M. Higley and set to music by his friend Daniel E. Kelley. Many versions followed, including this one by John Lomax in 1910. Settlers and cowboys loved it, and it became the state song of Kansas in 1947.

It's a great melody to sing and somehow so American, though this has never got in the way of my enthusiasm for singing it. I guess you just put on your imaginary chaps and get transported in your mind's eye to the plains of Arizona, Kansas or Oklahoma (ideally ignoring, just for a moment, the tragic history of the native men whose territorial issues are touched on in the third verse).

Oh, give me a home where the buffalo roam,
Where the deer and the antelope play,
Where seldom is heard a discouraging word
And the skies are not cloudy all day.

Home, home on the range,
Where the deer and the antelope play,
Where seldom is heard a discouraging word
And the skies are not cloudy all day.

Where the air is so pure, the zephyrs so free,
The breezes so balmy and light
That I would not exchange my home on the range
For all of the cities so bright.
Chorus

The red man was pressed from this part of the West;
He's likely no more to return
To the banks of Red River, where seldom if ever
Their flickering campfires burn.
Chorus

How often at night, when the heavens are bright
With the light from the glittering stars,
Have I stood here amazed, and asked as I gazed
If their glory exceeds that of ours.
Chorus

On Top of Old Smokey

YES, YES, we all know this one: 'On top of spaghetti, / All covered with cheese, / I lost my poor meatball / When somebody sneezed.' But it's a beautiful, very old traditional song with many different versions, thought to have travelled to America with the Scots-Irish who settled in the Appalachians. If you like this one, a similar tune is 'Down in the Valley', which then leads you to the 'Connemara Cradle Song'. Old songs very often have these 'siblings'.

On top of Old Smokey,
All covered with snow,
I lost my true lover,
For courting too slow.

For courting's a pleasure,
But parting is grief,
And a false-hearted lover
Is worse than a thief.

A thief will just rob you
And take what you have,
But a false-hearted lover
Will lead you to your grave.

The grave will decay you
And turn you to dust.
Not one boy in a hundred
A poor girl can trust.

They'll hug you and kiss you
And tell you more lies
Than crossties on a railroad
Or stars in the sky.

So come, ye young maidens,
And listen to me,
Never place your affection
In a green willow tree.

For the leaves they will wither,
The roots they will die,
And you'll be forsaken
And never know why.

Yankee Doodle

THE ORIGIN of this tune is unconfirmed, but it could be related to the English song 'Lucy Locket', about a lady of loose morals. Early versions of the melody appeared in the late-eighteenth-century book *Aird's Selection of Scotch, English, Irish and Foreign Airs*, and it was adopted by the British Army during the War of Independence, with verses ridiculing New Englanders. It's funny that this song, which once mocked dishevelled and undisciplined US soldiers, is now the state song of Connecticut and sung by all Americans with pride.

Could the word 'doodle' be derived from the Low German '*dudel*', which means 'fool', or from 'tootling' on a flute? And does 'macaroni' mean 'low class' or is it a term for a dandy? 'Yankee' may have come from the Cherokee Indian word '*eankke*', meaning 'coward', though linguistic research doesn't support this theory.

Just as in the song 'Shenandoah' (which follows in the next chapter), there is an endless choice of verses – you could sing these songs for hours.

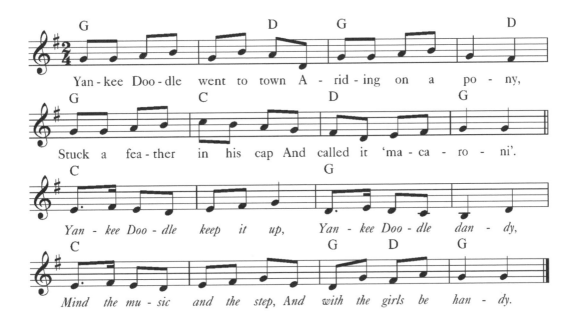

Yankee Doodle went to town
A-riding on a pony,
Stuck a feather in his cap
And called it 'macaroni'.

Yankee Doodle keep it up,
Yankee Doodle dandy,
Mind the music and the step,
And with the girls be handy.

Father and I went down to camp,
Along with Captain Gooding,
And there we saw the men and boys
As thick as hasty pudding.
Chorus

And there we saw a thousand men
As rich as Squire David,
And what they wasted every day,
I wish it could be saved.
Chorus

There was Captain Washington,
Upon a slapping stallion,
Giving orders to his men –
I guess there were a million.
Chorus

And then the feathers on his head,
They looked so very fine, ah,
I wanted peskily to get
To give to my Jemima.
Chorus

Skip to My Lou

THIS POPULAR partner-stealing dance comes from America's frontier period, when settlers expanded westwards across the country (from the seventeenth to the twentieth century). Instruments like the fiddle were considered the Devil's playthings and banned in many Protestant communities, so clapping songs were devised to take their place. People would clap the rhythm, sing and dance, and so they (especially the youngsters) had an outlet for their high spirits and could still socialize and enjoy music and dancing. 'Loo', a Scottish word for 'love', gradually evolved into 'Lou' as the song became Americanized.

This is equal to 'Peter Peck' as a tongue twister as far as I'm concerned. Singing 'shoo, fly, shoo' gives me enormous problems, no matter how hard I try.

ACTIONS

Hold hands with your partner, and join other couples skipping around in a ring. A single boy in the centre of this circle sings 'Lost my partner, what'll I do?' as the couples whirl past him. He decides which girl to choose, as he sings the various verses of the song. When he's ready, he takes the hand of the girl of his choice, her partner takes his place in the centre of the ring and the game continues.

Skip, skip, skip to my Lou,
Skip, skip, skip to my Lou,
Skip, skip, skip to my Lou,
Skip to my Lou, my darlin'.

Lost my partner, what'll I do?
Lost my partner, what'll I do?
Lost my partner, what'll I do?
Skip to my Lou, my darlin'.

I'll get another one, prettier than you . . .

Fly's in the buttermilk, shoo, fly, shoo . . .

There's a little red wagon, paint it blue . . .

Can't get a red bird, Jay bird'll do . . .

Cat's in the cream jar, ooh, ooh, ooh . . .

Off to Texas, Two by two . . .

When the Saints Go Marching In

ON PLANTATIONS in the American South, provocation could result in a severe beating or lashing for a slave. Even their worship and their songs were censored. 'Thus their symbolism became all the more evocative, cryptic, and intense, communicating to all those who were oppressed the hopeful message that they would one day be free and their oppressors punished' (Alan Lomax, *Folk Songs of North America* (1960)). This song is a great example, taking its imagery from the Book of Revelation: Gabriel's trumpets announcing the last judgement, the number of people to be redeemed from Earth and the world revealed ... no wonder it's become popular in New Orleans as a funeral song.

OPTION

Try singing this in a call-and-answer style

Oh, when the saints go marching in,
Oh, when the saints go marching in,
Oh Lord, I want to be in that number
When the saints go marching in.

Oh, when the revelation comes,
Oh, when the revelation comes,
Oh, I long to be in that number
When the saints go marching in.

And when the sun refuse to shine ...

Oh, when the moon turns red with blood ...

And when the earth has turned to fire ...

And when the new world is revealed ...

Oh, when they gather round the throne ...

And when they crown him King of Kings ...

And on that hallelujah day ...

Oh, when the trumpet sounds the call ...

This Train

THIS TRADITIONAL gospel song was first recorded in 1925 by Wood's Famous Blind Jubilee Singers. Electric-guitar-toting Sister Rosetta Tharpe does a great version.

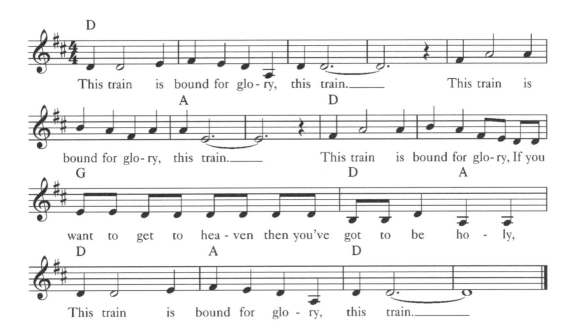

This train is bound for glory, this train.
This train is bound for glory, this train.
This train is bound for glory,
If you want to get to heaven then you've got
  to be holy,
This train is bound for glory, this train.

This train don't carry no gamblers, this train.
This train don't carry no gamblers, this train.
This train don't carry no gamblers,
No crap shooters, no midnight ramblers,
This train is bound for glory, this train.

This train is built for speed now, this train.
This train is built for speed now, this train.
This train is built for speed now,
Fastest train you ever did see,
This train is bound for glory, this train.

This train don't carry no liars, this train.
This train don't carry no liars, this train.
This train don't carry no liars,
No hypocrites and no high-flyers,
This train is bound for glory, this train.

This train don't carry no jokers, this train.
This train don't carry no jokers, this train.
This train don't carry no jokers,
No high-tone women, no cigar smokers,
This train is bound for glory, this train.

This train don't carry no rustlers, this train.
This train don't carry no rustlers, this train.
This train don't carry no rustlers,
Sidestreet walkers, two-bit hustlers,
This train is bound for glory, this train.

Joshua Fought the Battle of Jericho

THIS African-American spiritual from the nineteenth century is based on the biblical story of Joshua leading the Israelites into battle against Canaan. It's another song full of symbolic reference to escape and freedom – 'and the walls came tumbling down'.

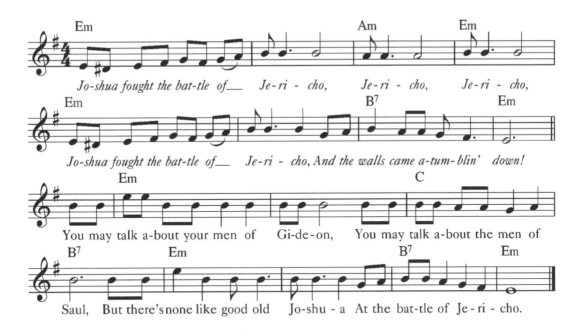

Joshua fought the battle of Jericho,
Jericho, Jericho,
Joshua fought the battle of Jericho,
And the walls came a-tumblin' down!

You may talk about your men of Gideon,
You may talk about the men of Saul,
But there's none like good old Joshua
At the battle of Jericho.
Chorus

Up to the walls of Jericho
They marched with spears in hand.
'Come blow them ram horns,' Joshua said,
''Cause the battle is in our hands.'
Chorus

Then the lamb, ram, sheep horns began to blow,
And the trumpets began to sound.
Joshua commanded the children to shout
And the walls came a-tumblin' down.
Chorus × 2

Will the Circle Be Unbroken?

THE EARLIEST version of this hymn (published in 1907) is credited to Ada R. Habershon (lyrics) and Charles H. Gabriel (music). It was amended by A. P. Carter, of The Carter Family, and the following lyric (from their 1935 recording) has become the most familiar. The tune is very similar to the Negro spiritual 'Glory, Glory (Since I Laid My Burden Down)'. This was one of the first songs I learned when I went to live in my hut in the hills of Tennessee.

Families used to sit around in circles, and when a family member died the circle was 'broken'. The song calls people to the altar to be saved, to be freed from sin so they could go to heaven and make the circle whole again.

I was standing by the window
On one cold and cloudy day,
And I saw the hearse come rolling
For to carry my mother away.

Can the circle be unbroken
By and by, Lord, by and by?
There's a better home a-waiting
In the sky, Lord, in the sky.

Lord, I told the undertaker,
Undertaker, please drive slow
For this body you are hauling,
How I hate to see her go.
Chorus

I followed close beside her,
Tried to hold up and be brave,
But I could not hide my sorrow
When they laid her in the grave.
Chorus

Went back home, Lord, my home was
  lonesome;
Missed my mother, she was gone.
All my brothers, sisters crying,
What a home, so sad and lone.
Chorus

Swing Low, Sweet Chariot

THIS SONG was written by Wallace Willis (also spelled Wallis Willis) around 1860. He was a black slave living in the Choctaw Nation area of Indian Territory (later Oklahoma), and also wrote 'Steal Away'. It's another fine example of a yearning-for-freedom spiritual. Some folklorists have even suggested that the title could be read as 'Swing low, sweet Harriet' – a plea to Harriet Tubman, one of the most successful 'conductors' on the Underground Railroad, the abolitionist network which helped hundreds of slaves find their way north to freedom during the nineteenth century. A friend of abolitionist John Brown (see p. 64), she escaped slavery in 1849 and went on to help more than seventy others escape too, reportedly forcing the timid ahead with a revolver!

I include this one with great pleasure – although some rugby fans may be surprised, it being so closely associated with the men in white, not the red of my home team … But first and foremost, it's a Negro spiritual, and a wonderful one at that. Paul Robeson's version is a favourite of mine. Here are the traditional lyrics.

Swing low, sweet chariot,
Coming for to carry me home,
Swing low, sweet chariot,
Coming for to carry me home.

I looked over Jordan, and what did I see
Coming for to carry me home?
A band of angels coming after me,
Coming for to carry me home.
Chorus

Sometimes I'm up, and sometimes I'm down,
(Coming for to carry me home)
But still my soul feels heavenly bound.
(Coming for to carry me home)
Chorus

The brightest day that I can say,
(Coming for to carry me home)
When Jesus washed my sins away.
(Coming for to carry me home)
Chorus

If I get there before you do,
(Coming for to carry me home)
I'll cut a hole and pull you through.
(Coming for to carry me home)
Chorus

If you get there before I do,
(Coming for to carry me home)
Tell all my friends I'm coming too.
(Coming for to carry me home)
Chorus

Goodnight, Irene

THE ORIGINS of this folk song are unclear, though it probably dates from the 1800s. It was first recorded in 1933 by Huddie Ledbetter ('Lead Belly'), a man with a fantastic ear for a good tune. He is famous for negotiating (with the help of a then-eighteen-year-old Alan Lomax) his way out of prison with this song.

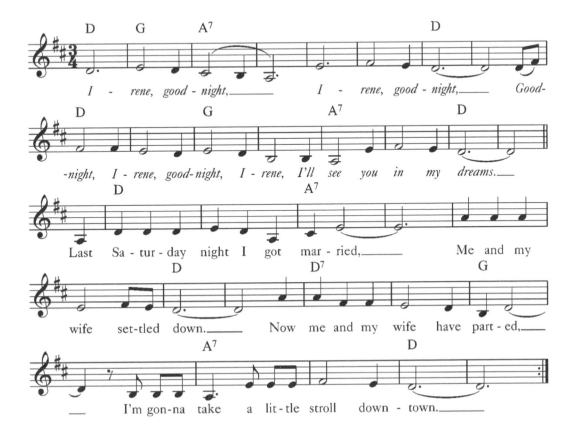

Irene, goodnight,
Irene, goodnight,
Goodnight, Irene, goodnight, Irene,
I'll see you in my dreams.

Last Saturday night I got married,
Me and my wife settled down.
Now me and my wife have parted,
I'm gonna take a little stroll downtown.
Chorus

Sometimes I live in the country,
Sometimes I live in town,
Sometimes I take a great notion
To jump in the river and drown.
Chorus

Quit your rambling, quit your gambling,
Stop staying out late at night.
Stay home with your wife and family
And stay by the fireside of right.
Chorus × 2

Little Boxes

POPULARIZED by folk giant Pete Seeger, this song was written by Malvina Reynolds when she was travelling from her home in Berkeley through San Francisco to Honda, for a meeting. Apparently, as she and her husband drove through Daly City, she said, 'Bud, take the wheel. I feel a song coming on.'

I learned it from a French boy who came to my school. This song was the only English he knew, and I've loved it ever since, first because of its catchy melody (and the French accent I hear it in), and then, in later life, because of the simplicity of the lyrics, carrying with them their wry political commentary.

Little boxes on the hillside,
Little boxes made of ticky tacky,
Little boxes on the hillside,
Little boxes all the same.
There's a green one and a pink one
And a blue one and a yellow one,
And they're all made out of ticky tacky
And they all look just the same.

And the people in the houses
All went to the university,
Where they were put in boxes
And they came out all the same,
And there's doctors and lawyers,
And business executives,
And they're all made out of ticky tacky
And they all look just the same.

And they all play on the golf course
And drink their martinis dry,
And they all have pretty children
And the children go to school,
And the children go to summer camp
And then to the university,
Where they are put in boxes
And they come out all the same.

And the boys go into business
And marry and raise a family
In boxes made of ticky tacky
And they all look just the same.
There's a green one and a pink one
And a blue one and a yellow one,
And they're all made out of ticky tacky
And they all look just the same.

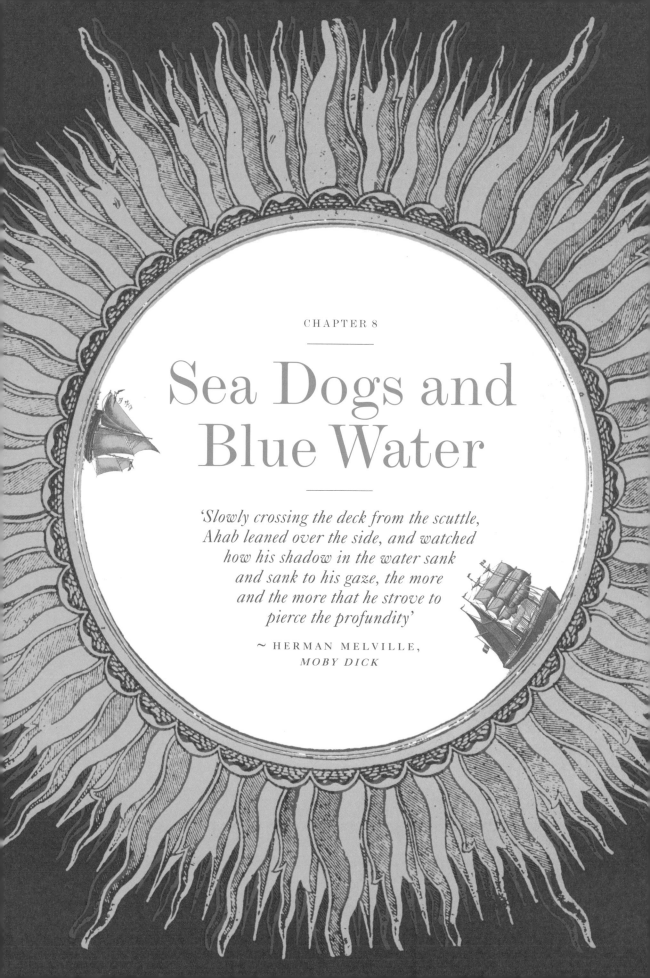

CHAPTER 8

Sea Dogs and Blue Water

*'Slowly crossing the deck from the scuttle,
Ahab leaned over the side, and watched
how his shadow in the water sank
and sank to his gaze, the more
and the more that he strove to
pierce the profundity'*

~ HERMAN MELVILLE,
MOBY DICK

NASHVILLE IS A LANDLOCKED TOWN, so when I had the urge to clear my head (which I would usually do by heading for the sea) I had two options: either go to the giant Bass Pro store along Opry Mills Drive, with its aquariums of giant albino catfish, acres of hunting gear and noise limiters for gun-toting babies, or visit the zoo, an oasis of 4x4-free calm in the company of soccer-playing elephants.

I missed open water and hankered after marching along the edge of cliffs, or heading off into the wind on a day's fishing along the coast. So occasionally I'd go off-shore fishing near Edisto Island, South Carolina. The wildlife was stunning — the mahi-mahi (also known as dolphinfish) were iridescent blue, green, yellow and turquoise, the crabs were bright blue, and the most magical of all were the flying fish journeying alongside the boat through and over the clear waters of the Atlantic Ocean. They whirr as they skim over the surface, like aquatic hummingbirds. The sun beats down and you could be living in a Tolkien novel. River and creek fishing have their exotic looking inhabitants too — giant dragonflies and translucent shrimp.

Nature's poetry lends itself so easily to song, and open water, the sea, the ocean, rivers, ships and sailing all make ideal metaphors or subjects for songs — 'The Water is Wide', 'Wade in the Water', 'Down by the Riverside', 'River Deep — Mountain High' ... and there are plenty of water-related songs of escape, migration, exploration, adventure, romance, industry, whimsy and religion. This chapter is that watery one.

What Shall We Do with the Drunken Sailor?

IT'S THE most well-known sea shanty of all – a quick one too, as shanties go – sung to aid large crews as they did hard tasks that necessitated working in time together for maximum efficiency, like hauling rope to raise the sails, or turning the vessel. The air is a traditional Irish dance, and the song may be American though nobody can find evidence to corroborate this. There's a version in 'Incidents of a Whaling Voyage' (1839), not much different from the version here.

It has been called a 'stamp 'n' go' song. Sing it 'earl-eye in the morning', like Burl Ives.

OPTIONS

Change the drunk:

'What shall we do with the Queen o' Sheba?'

'What shall we do with the Virgin Mary?'

'What'll we do with a Limejuice skipper?'
('Soak him in oil till he sprouts a flipper.')

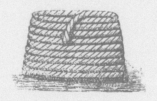

What shall we do with the drunken
    sailor,
What shall we do with the drunken
    sailor,
What shall we do with the drunken
    sailor,
Early in the morning?

Weigh heigh and up she rises,
Weigh heigh and up she rises,
Weigh heigh and up she rises,
Early in the morning.

Put him in the long boat till he's sober ...

Put him in the scuppers with a hosepipe
    on him ...

Take 'im an' shake 'im an' try an' wake
    'im ...

Scrape the hair off his chest with a hoop-
    iron razor ...

Give 'im a dose of salt and water ...

Put him in bed with the captain's daughter ...

The *John B.* Sails

THIS ONE'S an old West Indian song. Have a listen to Alan Lomax's 1935 recording of it, called 'Histe up the *John B.* Sail' with the Cleveland Simmons Group, for a more island feel to the phrasing. The Beach Boys had a global hit with their version ('Sloop *John B.*'), and it is sung all too often in a home-returning vehicle after a day's sport.

We come on the sloop *John B.*, My grand-fa - ther and me, A-round Nas-sau town we_ did roam; Drink-ing all night, we got in-to a fight,_____ And we feel so break-up, we want to go home._____

We come on the sloop *John B.*,
My grandfather and me,
Around Nassau town we did roam;
Drinking all night, we got into a fight,
And we feel so break-up, we want to go
    home.

So h'ist up the John B. *sails,*
See how the mainsail set,
Then send for the captain – shore, let us go
    home,
I want to go home, let me go home,
I feel so broke-up, I want to go home.

The first mate he got drunk
And broke in the Cap'n's trunk,
The constable had to come and take him
    away.
Sheriff John Stone, why don't you leave me
    alone, yeah, yeah,
Well, I feel so broke up, I want to go home.
Chorus

De poor cook he got fits,
Tro' 'way all de grits,
Den he took an' eat up all o' my corn!
Lemme go home, why don't they let me go
    home?
Dis is de worst trip since I been born!
    [or 'I ever been on!']
Chorus

The Ash Grove

NOT THE Ash Grove Folk Music Club found at 8162 Melrose Avenue in Los Angeles, where Lightnin' Hopkins, Mississippi John Hurt and Ry Cooder played, but the song it was named after. It is one of Wales' most familiar and beloved songs, first appearing in a book by harpist Edward Jones in 1802 – although a similar tune appears much earlier (1728) in John Gay's *Beggar's Opera* (his 'Cease Your Funning' song).

Children all over the UK sing their own versions, like this one:

Oh, [insert name] is a funny 'un,
Got a face like a pickled onion,
A nose like a squashed tomato,
And feet like flat fish.

My favourite version is in Welsh, by Gerallt Jones, about an old sea captain who retires from a life at sea to go and live with his love, Gwen of Llwyn Onn:

Henceforth I will quietly navigate
  by my Gwen,
In the small ship of our cottage
  with her at the helm …

But here's the most well-known version in English, written by John Oxenford in the nineteenth century.

The ash grove, how graceful, how plainly 'tis speaking,
The harp through its playing has language for me.
Whenever the light through its branches is breaking
A host of kind faces is gazing on me.
The friends from my childhood again are before me,
Each step wakes a memory as freely I roam.
With soft whispers laden the leaves rustle o'er me,
The ash grove, the ash grove alone is my home.

Down yonder green valley where streamlets meander
When twilight is fading I pensively rove,
Or at the bright noon tide in solitude wander
Amid the dark shades of the lonely ash grove.
'Twas there while the blackbird was cheerfully singing
I first met that dear one, the joy of my heart.
Around us for gladness the bluebells were ringing
But then little thought I how soon we should part.

One, Two, Three, Four, Five

ONE 80S SUMMER along the Mumbles Mile (where open-decked tram buses would have rumbled along twenty years earlier), you might have seen a rah-rah-skirted roller-skating tweener dragging a dead fish on a lead. It was a dogfish, mottled and sandy and gruesome looking, but passers-by were stopped and ask to name this 'pet'. 'It's an old shoe,' said one, with a heavy lisp, a phrase which made my day. I dragged it home and gave it sanctuary in the rusting bowl of the concrete mixer which had taken root in the garden. It stank for long hot days, then I forgot about it.

Moral? Dead fish are as much fun as catching live ones.

This is a traditional English traditional rhyme, first published in *Mother Goose's Melody* around 1765. It used to be about a hare:

One, two, three, four and five,
I caught a hare alive;
Six, seven, eight, nine and ten,
I let him go again.

But the animal became a fish, and a second stanza was added in the 1800s. It's a song I check voice levels through microphones (as a change from the usual 'What I had for breakfast was …')

One, two, three, four, five,
Once I caught a fish alive.
Six, seven, eight, nine, ten,
Then I let it go again.
Why did you let it go?
Because it bit my finger so.
Which finger did it bite?
This little finger on my right.

Down by the Riverside

THIS AMERICAN spiritual (also known as 'Study War No More') was first transcribed in the years following the Civil War. Pete Seeger and The Weavers revived it in the 1950s, and it became popular as an anti-violence, anti-war song in the 1960s. In primary school, we sang a much lighter-weight version about stealing kisses down by the seaside, which I found quite risqué at the age of eight.

Great versions worth checking out are those by Snooks Eaglin, Louis Armstrong, Mahalia Jackson and Sister Rosetta Tharpe – they are all infectious.

ACTIONS

Try singing harmonies, and also a 'call and response' version – you sing the first line, and others answer you with the 'Down by the riverside' response. Add off-beat claps and a tambourine and hey presto! You 'is a Southern church'. 'Amen' for three minutes at least.

Gonna lay down my sword and shield
Down by the riverside,
Down by the riverside,
Down by the riverside.
Gonna lay down my sword and shield
Down by the riverside.
Ain't gonna study war no more.

I ain't gonna study war no more,
I ain't gonna study war no more,
Study war no more.
I ain't gonna study war no more,
I ain't gonna study war no more,
Study war no more.

Gonna stick my sword in the golden sand …
Chorus

Gonna put on my long white robe …
Chorus

Gonna put on my starry crown …
Chorus

Gonna put on my golden shoes …
Chorus

Gonna talk with the Prince of Peace …
Chorus

Gonna shake hands around the world …
Chorus

Shenandoah

THIS SONG speaks with that universal voice that great poems possess. Any singer can identify with and be touched by the yearning in the melody and lyrics of the song, wherever they're from.

It's an American sea shanty, popular during the migration West in the nineteenth century. Escaping slaves were also said to have loved 'Shenandoah', as the river hid their scent. This is a version from 1910, collected by W. B. Whall, a master mariner. It tells the story of an illicit love affair between a white man and an Indian girl. There are many versions, and many, many verses – over seventy at the last count!

Oh, Shenandoah, I long to hear you,
Away, you rolling river,
Oh, Shenandoah, I long to hear you,
Ah-ha, I'm bound away
'Cross the wide Missouri.

Missouri, she's a mighty river,
Away, you rolling river,
The red-skins' camp lies on its borders.
Ah-ha, I'm bound away,
'Cross the wide Missouri.

The white man loved the Indian maiden,
Away, you rolling river,
With notions* his canoe was laden.
Ah-ha, I'm bound away,
'Cross the wide Missouri.

'Oh, Shenandoah, I love your daughter,
Away, you rolling river,
I'll take her 'cross yon rolling water.'
Ah-ha, I'm bound away,
'Cross the wide Missouri.

The chief disdained the trader's dollars:
Away, you rolling river,
'My daughter never you shall follow.'
Ah-ha, I'm bound away,
'Cross the wide Missouri.

'Oh, Shenandoah, I long to hear you,
Away, you rolling river.
Across that wide and rolling river.'
Ah-ha, I'm bound away,
'Cross the wide Missouri.

[* 'notions' = knick-knacks]

My Bonnie Lies Over the Ocean

THIS IS A very easy song to learn, and so despite it being quite over sung, I've decided that it should stay. If you think of it as an old seafaring song, or as a smooth, pulsing lullaby like the 'Connemara Cradle Song' ('On the wings of the wind, O'er the dark rolling sea, Angels are coming to watch over thee, So list to the wind coming over the sea … Flag your head over, and Hear the wind blow…'), then you can learn to love it again.

The origins of this folk song are unknown, though it is thought to be Scottish. Could the 'Bonnie' in the song be a man? Could it be about Bonnie Prince Charlie?

My Bonnie lies over the ocean,
My Bonnie lies over the sea,
My Bonnie lies over the ocean,
O, bring back my Bonnie to me.

Bring back, bring back,
O, bring back my Bonnie to me, to me;
Bring back, bring back,
O, bring back my Bonnie to me.

O, blow ye winds over the ocean,
O, blow ye winds over the sea.
O, blow ye winds over the ocean,
And bring back my Bonnie to me.
Chorus

Last night as I lay on my pillow,
Last night as I lay on my bed,
Last night as I lay on my pillow,
I dreamed that my Bonnie was dead.
Chorus

The winds have blown over the ocean,
The winds have blown over the sea,
The winds have blown over the ocean,
And brought back my Bonnie to me.
Chorus

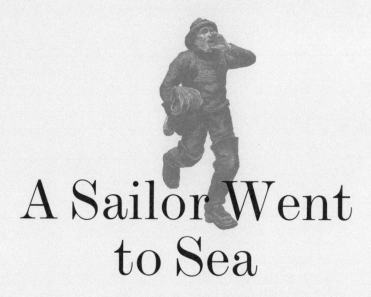

A Sailor Went to Sea

THIS IS A clapping game (or for jumping rope). There are some very funny hokum songs with similarly unfinished lines made to lead the listener to fill in the bawdy word that rhymes. This one, however, is not X-rated.

ACTIONS

Clap your hands together, then hit your partner's right hand (palms together) with yours. Clap your own hands together again, then hit your partner's left hand with yours. And repeat.

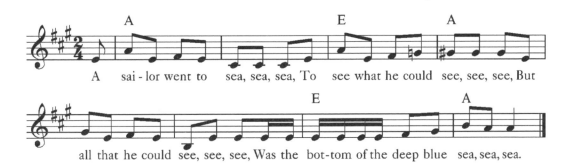

A sai - lor went to sea, sea, sea, To see what he could see, see, see, But all that he could see, see, see, Was the bot-tom of the deep blue sea, sea, sea.

A sailor went to sea, sea, sea,
To see what he could see, see, see,
But all that he could see, see, see,
Was the bottom of the deep blue sea, sea, sea.

Oh, Helen had a steamboat,
The steamboat had a bell.
When Helen went to heaven,
The steamboat went to —.

Hello, operator,
Just give me number nine.
If the line is busy,
I'll kick your big —.

Behind the old piano
There was a piece of glass.
Helen slipped upon it
And hurt her little —.

Ask me for a muffin,
I'll give you some old bread,
And if you do not like it,
Just go and soak your —.

Down By the River Liv'd a Maiden

(Oh My Darling, Clementine)

WRITTEN by H. S. Thompson and published in 1863, this song is the basis for Percy Montrose's 'Oh My Darling, Clementine' (1884). In some versions of

'Clementine' the mourning lover gets over his loss by immediately finding love with her sister, which seems rather a short mourning. I prefer the older version, warning against the dangers of drinking near water, which is a moral missed by many lake-going folk in Tennessee. House boats (large floating boxes) are really floating bars, and Pabst Blue Ribbons, rum and cokes, all-angle baseball caps and jet skis are all you need for your red-neck holiday. But keep this song in mind. I saved a woman's life once on one of these days out: a very drunk lady lurched and fell over the side of her boat and disappeared under the water before any of her also very 'spirited' companions had noticed. I fished her out. I don't think she noticed either.

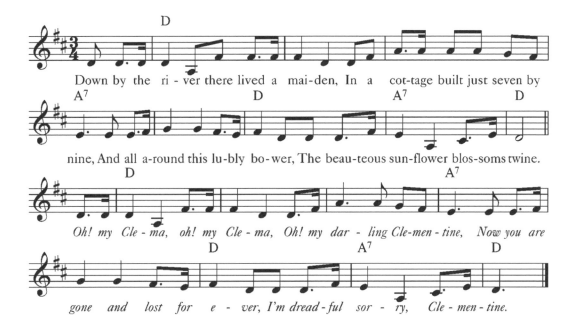

Down by the ri - ver there lived a mai-den, In a cot-tage built just seven by nine, And all a-round this lu-bly bo-wer, The beau-teous sun-flower blos-soms twine. Oh! my Cle - ma, oh! my Cle - ma, Oh! my dar - ling Cle-men - tine, Now you are gone and lost for e - ver, I'm dread-ful sor - ry, Cle - men - tine.

Down by the river there lived a maiden,
In a cottage built just seven by nine,
And all around this lubly bower,
The beauteous sunflower blossoms twine.

Oh! my Clema, oh! my Clema,
Oh! my darling Clementine,
Now you are gone and lost forever,
I'm dreadful sorry, Clementine.

One day de wind was blowing awful,
I took her down some old rye wine,
And listened to de sweetest cooings
Ob my sweet sunflower Clementine.
Chorus

De ducks had gone done to de riber,
To drive dem back she did incline,
She stubb'd her toe and Oh! Kersliver,
She fell into the foamy brine.
Chorus

I see'd her lips above de waters,
A blowing bubbles bery fine,
But 'turnt no use, I wa'n't no swimmer,
And so I lost my Clementine.
Chorus

Now all young men by me take warning,
Don't gib your ladies too much rye wine,
Kase like as not in this wet wedder
Dey'll share de fate ob Clementine.
Chorus

Fraulein

I LEARNED a song once, in a pitch-black night on a tiny island: no electricity, just sand, black greenery and the shell of a Japanese fighter plane from the Second World War in the sea. I was in Butaritari, in the Pacific Ocean. 'Bromine, bromine, oh, where have you been?' went the chorus. I looked for the song on my return and it turned out to be this American country song about a German girl: 'Fraulein'. Like a game of Chinese Whispers, the song had changed somewhat as it flew to its nest where I'd heard it, three degrees north of the equator. Just humming this melody takes me back to that black, black night on a faraway atoll.

The song, written by Lawton Williams, was released by Bobby Helms in 1957.

Far across deep blue waters lives an old
   German's daughter
By the banks of the old river Rhine
Where I loved her and left her, but I can't
   forget her,
'Cause I miss my pretty fraulein.

Fraulein, Fraulein, look up toward the Heaven
Each night when the stars start to shine,
By the same stars above you, I swear that I love
   you,
You are my pretty fraulein.

When my memories wander, away over
   yonder
To the sweetheart that I left behind,
In a moment of glory, a face comes before
   me,
The face of my pretty fraulein.
Chorus

Fraulein, Fraulein, walk down by the river,
Pretend that your hand's holdin' mine,
By the same stars above you, I swear that
   I love you
'Cause you are my pretty fraulein.
Chorus

CHAPTER 9

Creature Songs

'I am fond of pigs. Dogs look up to us.
Cats look down on us. Pigs treat us as equals'

~ WINSTON CHURCHILL

ARE YOU A CAT OR DOG PERSON? What a potty question that is. But I'm going to take it a little further. I'm a plant person. I had a great biology teacher at school, who would nag people about eyesight and badger everyone into getting spectacles. She was right about my eyes — I was short-sighted. But when it came to botany — phloem and xylem, photosynthesis, symbiotic relationships, osmosis and stomata — it all became clear and I loved it. At home, I grew marrows, rhubarb and apples, all easy and giving plants. My bedroom was a jungle. You might have once found in the corner of my room a pickling jar. It had in it an African tree frog that I'd found in a box of bananas at the fruit stall I worked at in Swansea Market as a Saturday girl. The frog died in a blink while my plants thrived. When we started the band I'd try, if there was any land or sunny bit of concrete available at our bedsit, to grow some greenery. But when the band took off, touring took its toll on the topiary.

There are, of course, some great stories involving animals. One which is told as a true story but is rooted in that more mysterious place, the imagination, is this heart-wrenching tale, familiar to many cultures although the animals differ. In India it's a snake and a mongoose, in Egypt a servant and a snake, in Malaysia a tame bear and a tiger. In Wales it's a dog and a wolf, and the dog's name is Gelert, the favourite hound of a prince who is the proud new father of a baby. He returns from a hunting trip to find the cot empty, the room and hound covered in blood. Thinking the hound had killed his baby, the prince slays him, only to find the dead body of a wolf lying nearby and the baby safe and well. It's strange to hear stories of wolves now — the way they were persecuted to extinction across almost all of Europe during the last millennium makes for fascinating reading. But let's return to the songs, and a whole chapter dedicated to wee little furry, feathered and squirmy creatures.

211

Chick, Chick, Chicken

WRITTEN BY Fred Holt, Thomas McGhee and Irving King, this song was released by many bands, including Harry Rester's Six Jumping Jacks in 1926. In their version, a trumpeter mimics a chicken. When I sing it, I can't help being reminded of the 'eat eggs' campaign run by the British Egg Marketing Board in the 50s and 60s. Fay Weldon was behind the slogan 'Go to work on an egg'. There was also 'Soldiering on', and one which was such a tongue twister that I don't remember it clearly, just that it was about eggs and was emblazoned on some sticky tape I had.

OPTION

'Easter' is sometimes replaced by 'breakfast'.

Chick, chick, chick, chick, chicken,
Lay a little egg for me.
Chick, chick, chick, chick, chicken,
I want one for my tea.
I haven't had an egg since Easter,
And now it's half past three
So, chick, chick, chick, chick, chicken,
Lay a little egg for me.

Run Rabbit Run

THIS SONG was written by Noel Gay and Ralph Butler for the 1939 show 'The Little Dog Laughed'.

I once bought a rabbit from Portobello Market and put it in the freezer till my dad (also a lover of game) came to stay. My husband is vegetarian, our nine-year-old is vegetarian and our seven-year-old is sensitive but I hadn't expected the opening of the freezer would result in mass tears. I cooked the rabbit when they were all out, but it wasn't an enjoyable meal after that. Here's my deal: I don't eat factory-farmed meat and I rarely buy meat to cook in the house. I don't like the taste of processed food but I like the occasional quail, and I love an occasional pheasant. And rabbits taste good once a year. So let me eat rabbit, and let there be no tears.

OPTION

This was Churchill's favourite song during the Blitz; the lyrics were changed to poke fun at Hitler:

Run Adolf, run Adolf, run, run, run,
Now that the fun has begun, gun, gun;
P'raps you'll just allow us to explain,
What we did once – we can do again.
We're making shells by the ton, ton, ton.
We've got the men and the mon, mon, mon.
Poor old soul, you'll need a rabbit hole,
So, run Adolf, run Adolf, run, run, run.

On the farm, every Friday,
On the farm, it's rabbit pie day.
So, every Friday that ever comes along,
I get up early and sing this little song.

Run rabbit, run rabbit
— Run! Run! Run!
Run rabbit, run rabbit
— Run! Run! Run!
Bang! Bang! Bang! Bang!
Goes the farmer's gun.
Run rabbit, run rabbit
— Run! Run! Run! Run!

Run rabbit, run rabbit
— Run! Run! Run!
Don't give the farmer his fun! Fun! Fun!
He'll get by without his rabbit pie,
So run rabbit, run rabbit
— Run! Run! Run!

There's a Worm at the Bottom of My Garden

I LEARNED this song (origin unknown) in America too – land of butter substitute, cream substitutes, Honeybuns and Twinkies. Worms would be a much healthier option. The song reminds me of my hours of experimenting at the bottom of the garden, playing with worms and insects. And smoking leaves with that magnifying glass. Poor, poor insects. I even ate an earwig once…

Here's a rhyme to follow on the worm theme:

Nobody likes me,
Everybody hates me,
Guess I'll go eat worms.

Long, thin, slimy ones,
Short, fat, juicy ones,
Itsy bitsy, fuzzy wuzzy worms.

Down goes the first one,
Down goes the second one,
Oh, how they wiggle and squirm.

Up comes the first one,
Up comes the second one,
Oh, how they wiggle and squirm.

There's a worm at the bottom of my garden,
And his name is Wiggly Woo.
There's a worm at the bottom of my garden,
And all that he can do
Is wiggle all day and wiggle all night –
The neighbours say what a terrible fright!
There's a worm at the bottom of my garden,
And his name is Wiggly Woo!

Nellie the Elephant

THIS SONG, originally written by Ralph Butler and Peter Hart in 1956, was revived during the 1984 Christmas holidays when a fast-tempo version by The Toy Dolls got to number 4 in the UK charts. It has been used (note: not the punk version) to help people learn the correct rhythm for CPR (along with the Bee Gee's 'Stayin' Alive').

Hey Diddle Diddle

AS I'M writing this book, it's reported that Sarah Brightman spent some tens of millions on a trip to the moon. And Felix Baumgartner made a 24-mile jump and broke the sound barrier. An aeroplane passes my study window, lights flashing, and I shudder as I watch it rise steeply away from Heathrow. I don't like flying. I always imagine the worst, and I think the same at the edge of cliffs, ditto hearing the fine details of the physical realities of the Earth in the Universe – a one-inch change and we're doomed. This nursery rhyme is up there with all that. Unfathomable.

It's a very popular nonsense verse, first printed *c.* 1765 but references to it were made as early as 1569: 'they can play a new dance called hey-didle-didle' (Thomas Preston, in a 'lamentable tragedy mixed ful of pleasant mirth, conteyning the life of Cambises King of Persia'). There are lots of theories regarding its symbolic meaning, including possible references to various constellations, the Israelites' Flight from Egypt, Catherine of Aragon (Catherine la Fidèle), the old-time inn game of cat (trap ball) … the list continues, but none have been proven.

Hey did-dle did-dle, The Cat and the fid-dle, The Cow jumped o-ver the moon, The

lit-tle Dog laughed to see such sport, And the Dish ran a-way with the Spoon.

Hey diddle diddle,

The Cat and the fiddle,

The Cow jumped over the moon,

The little Dog laughed to see such sport,

And the Dish ran away with the Spoon.

Little Bo Peep

THIS IS AN English song, from about 1805, and it has some mysterious connotations. Sussex folklore claims a girl called Bo Peep as a local heroine, who used her sheep to disguise smugglers' footprints to help them escape.

Others see it as an allegory where 'sheep' = smugglers and 'tails' = contraband goods. Of course, it may simply be an old rhyme to teach children to be good to animals.

Little Bo-Peep has lost her sheep,
And doesn't know where to find them;
Leave them alone, and they'll come home,
Wagging their tails behind them.

Little Bo Peep fell fast asleep,
And dreamt she heard them bleating;
But when she awoke, she found it a joke,
For they were still all fleeting.

Then up she took her little crook,
Determined for to find them;
She found them indeed, but it made her heart bleed,
For they'd left their tails behind them.

It happened one day, as Bo-peep did stray
Into a meadow hard by,
There she espied their tails side by side,
All hung on a tree to dry.

She heaved a sigh and wiped her eye,
And over the hillocks went rambling,
And tried what she could, as a shepherdess should,
To tack each again to its lambkin.

Baa, Baa, Black Sheep

HERE'S ANOTHER English song, with printed sources dating back to the early eighteenth century, but possibly much earlier. It has been suggested that it refers to the medieval English wool tax of 1275, but also that it may be connected with the slave trade. Nobody knows!

OPTION

The rhyme is usually sung to a variant of the 1761 French melody 'Ah! Vous dirai-je, Maman' (also used for 'Twinkle, Twinkle, Little Star'). I've been saying for years that Mozart had composed 'Twinkle, Twinkle', which although not true has a grain of truth – he did compose twelve variations of this French folk tune. It's a cute one:

Ah! Vous dirai-je, Maman,	Ah! Shall I tell you, Mummy,
Ce qui cause mon tourment?	What is tormenting me?
Papa veut que je raisonne	Daddy wants me to reason
Comme une grande personne.	Like a grown-up person.
Moi, je dis que les bonbons	Me, I say that sweets
Valent mieux que la raison.	Are worth more than reason.

Baa, baa, black sheep,
Have you any wool?
Yes, sir, yes, sir,
Three bags full;
One for the master,
And one for the dame,
And one for the little boy
Who lives down the lane.

Hickory Dickory Dock

AND HERE'S another old English rhyme – an early version appears in 1744 in *Tommy Thumb's Pretty Song Book*: 'Hickere, Dickere, Dock'. Like 'Eenee Meenee Minee Mo', it was used to decide who begins a game. Sir Walter Scott recited a similar version: 'ziccoty, doccoty, dock', and it could have come from counting sheep in Westmoreland, where 'hevera' meant eight, 'devera' meant nine and 'dick' meant ten.

OPTION

You could make up new verses:

'The clock struck two,
The mouse went to the loo.'
'The clock struck ten,
The mouse came again.'

(this last example is a verse from 1863, but you get the idea ...)

Hickory, dickory, dock,
The mouse ran up the clock.
The clock struck one,
The mouse ran down,
Hickory, dickory, dock.

Three Blind Mice

THE EARLIEST version of this rhyme was published in 1609, possibly written by Thomas Ravenscroft, a male chorister at St Paul's Cathedral. It's a round song, so can be sung in canon form and never end …

A favourite theory is that it tells of Queen Mary's revenge on the clergy as she changed the country back to Catholicism from the Protestantism that her father, Henry VIII, had forcibly established. The three blind mice may refer to bishops Hugh Latimer, Nicholas Ridley and the Archbishop of Canterbury, Thomas Cranmer, and their execution. This would have been happening around 1553, when Mary ascended the throne. It's conjecture, but it's a good story and the dates match for once.

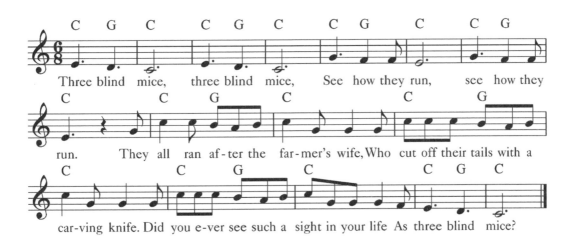

Three blind mice, three blind mice,
See how they run, see how they run.
They all ran after the farmer's wife,
Who cut off their tails with a carving knife.
Did you ever see such a sight in your life
As three blind mice?

Old MacDonald Had a Farm

VARIOUS SONGS which list animals and their noises like this date right back to the early 1700s.

This one is popular all over the world, with the farmer's name changing to suit the location – you'll find Grandpa Ali, Uncle Moshe, Uncle Manuel, Pepito, Hansen, Per Olsson, Old Mister Wang, Ichiro and Jiro amongst the farmers who work on that animal-filled farm. My aim for a long while when growing up was to marry a farmer and spend all my time up to my neck in slurry and milk. Doubts about the wisdom of this came one hungover morning, aged eighteen. 'Help!' shouted Mum, 'come out now!' so I did, and my head was soon at the bottom end of a pitifully bleating sheep. 'Get the maggots out,' said Mum. 'Maggots?!' I replied, 'Maggots?!' Indeed, blowfly had set in around the sheep's tail and I was to remove them with some strong chemical which on application to the affected area made living maggots crawl out of living sheep flesh.

This, crossed with a spinning Brynawelon-disco-morning head was enough to make me think twice about a career in farming. I did the job, and the sheep recovered, but bottoms have never seemed the same again.

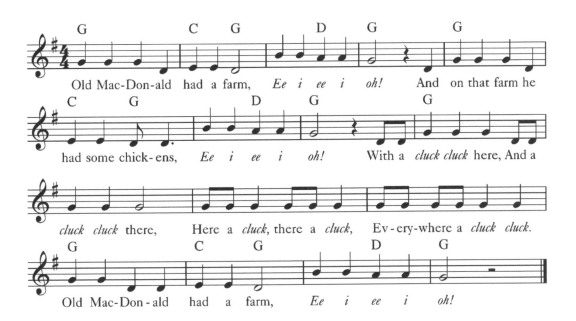

Old MacDonald had a farm,
Ee i ee i oh!
And on that farm he had some chickens,
Ee i ee i oh!
With a *cluck cluck* here,
And a *cluck cluck* there,
Here a *cluck*, there a *cluck*,
Everywhere a *cluck cluck*.
Old MacDonald had a farm,
Ee i ee i oh!

Old MacDonald had a farm,
Ee i ee i oh!
And on that farm he had some dogs,
Ee i ee i oh!
With a *woof woof* here,
And a *woof woof* there
Here a *woof*, there a *woof*,
Everywhere a *woof woof*.
Old MacDonald had a farm,
Ee i ee i oh!

Turkeys ... A *gobble gobble* here ...
Cows ... A *moo moo* here ...
Sheep ... A *baa baa* here ...
Horses ... A *neigh neigh* here ...
Pigs ... An *oink oink* here ...
Cats ... A *miaow miaow* here ...

The Quartermaster's Store

I WAS A short-sighted child: far-off objects a haze, numbers missing and words floating. My son has my genes – we took him to the optician's recently to fit his first pair. Not the NHS pink rims (later to be held together by a plaster) that I first wore, nor the salmon pink and amber round specs of the 80s, but handsome black metal ones. Squinting is what we do, and this song is perfect for us mole-eyed myopics. Add to that silly rhymes, harmony- and canon-singing potential and even its endlessness is forgiven. Here are plenty of verses to get on with, 'all through the night'.

There are rats, rats, rats, big as alley cats
In the store, in the store.
There are rats, rats, rats, big as alley cats
In the quartermaster's store.

My eyes are dim I cannot see,
I have not brought my specs with me.
I have not brought my specs with me.

Snakes ... big as garden rakes ...

Foxes ... stuffed in little boxes ...

Bears ... with curlers in their hair ...

Fleas ... crawling on our knees ...

Rac-rac-coons ... stealing all the spoons ...

Apes ... eating all the grapes ...

Bees ... with little knobby knees ...

Fishes ... washing all the dishes ...

Goats ... eating all the oats ...

Cakes ... that give us tummy aches ...

Butter ... running in the gutter ...

Cheese ... with kilts and hairy knees ...

Beans ... as big as submarines ...

Eggs ... with thick and hairy legs ...

Gravy ... enough to float the navy ...

Kippers ... in little furry slippers ...

CHAPTER 10

Sweet Dreams

*'I love sleep. My life has the tendency to
fall apart when I'm awake, you know?'*

~ ERNEST HEMINGWAY

I HAVE TWO MAJOR REGRETS. One is not filling in a form properly (I've a lifelong phobia of filling in forms) and missing out on Mother Maybelle's guitar, which had come up for auction from the Carter/Cash estate in 2004. The other came scarcely five weeks after the birth of my first child, Glenys. Lying on the bed, I felt inspired to write lullabies to her there on the spot. Minidisc on record, I sang for a full twenty minutes, improvising and weaving a medley of songs. The melodies just came without any real conscious effort. Glen slept; I left the room to listen back to what I had just sung. There was nothing recorded. My new microphone attachment had an on/off button, which had remained off — the songs were lost.

Those moments alone with a child or a fellow being as the sun cools and the night draws in, clean, warm and safe, day lived, story read, tucked in and ready for sleep are the most hopeful moments, and songs go hand in hand with those intimate and loving, trusting times ... Most songs, if you love them, can be slowed right down and made to fit bedtime. These are some of my favourites.

Over the Rainbow

THIS SONG was written by Harold Arlen (music) and E. Y. Harburg (lyrics) for the 1939 film *The Wizard of Oz*. Judy Garland said: '"Over the Rainbow" has become part of my life. It's so symbolic of everybody's dreams and wishes that I'm sure that's why some people get tears in their eyes when they hear it. I've sung it thousands of times and it's still the song that's closest to my heart.' It's ranked number 1 in the 'Songs of the Century' chart compiled by the Recording Industry Association of America and the National Endowment for the Arts. And it's also ranked the 'greatest film song of all time' on the American Film Institute's '100 Years ... 100 Songs' list. It's another song that was hugely popular amongst the soldiers fighting the Second World War.

Somewhere over the rainbow, way up high,
There's a land that I've heard of once in a
    lullaby.
Somewhere over the rainbow, skies are blue,
And the dreams that you dare to dream
Really do come true.

Someday I'll wish upon a star
And wake up where the clouds are far
Behind me.

Where troubles melt like lemon drops,
High above the chimney tops,
That's where you'll find me.

Somewhere over the rainbow, bluebirds fly.
Birds fly over the rainbow,
Why then, oh, why can't I?
If happy little bluebirds fly beyond the
    rainbow
Why, oh, why can't I?

When You Wish Upon a Star

WRITTEN BY Leigh Harline (music) and Ned Washington (lyrics) for Walt Disney's film adaptation of

Pinocchio (1940) – yes, it's another film classic bound to twang the heartstrings.

When you wish upon a star,
Makes no difference who you are,
Anything your heart desires
Will come to you.

If your heart is in your dream,
No request is too extreme,
When you wish upon a star
As dreamers do.

Fate is kind,
She brings to those who love
The sweet fulfilment of
Their secret longing.

Like a bolt out of the blue,
Fate steps in and sees you through',
When you wish upon a star
Your dreams come true.

Edelweiss

THIS ONE was included in the 1959 musical *The Sound of Music*, and it's a song from the immense partnership of melody-writer Richard Rodgers and lyric-writer Oscar Hammerstein. They also wrote such classics as *The King and I*, *South Pacific* and *Oklahoma!*

This song is guaranteed to get me bawling – such a tiny symbol of peace in this crazy, crazy world.

Edelweiss, edelweiss,
Ev'ry morning you greet me.
Small and white,
Clean and bright,
You look happy to meet me.

Blossom of snow
May you bloom and grow,
Bloom and grow for ever.
Edelweiss, edelweiss,
Bless my homeland for ever.

You Are My Sunshine

THIS SONG was first recorded by The Pine Ridge Boys in 1939; in 1940 Jimmie Davis bought the rights to it and thereafter claimed it as his own. It has since become one of the state songs of Louisiana through its associations with Davis, a former governor of the state.

Is it the best lullaby ever? Well, it's one that's very popular at bedtimes in our house. I always thought it was based on a traditional song, but I can't find any evidence to corroborate this nor to blow the theory.

You are my sunshine,
My only sunshine.
You make me happy
When skies are grey.
You'll never know, dear,
How much I love you,
So please don't take
My sunshine away.

The other night, dear,
As I lay sleeping
I dreamed I held you
In my arms.
When I awoke, dear,
I was mistaken
And I held my head and cried.

Rock-a-Bye Baby

COULD THIS have been the first poem written on US soil by a pilgrim, just arrived there on the *Mayflower*? The Opies' *Dictionary of Nursery Rhymes* contains a suggestion that it may derive from the use of wind to rock Native American cradles suspended from tree branches. Popular on both sides of the Atlantic, its true origins are unknown.

Toddlers bite. Toddlers throw things and they pull hair. I always associate this song with the violent jerking of a toddler trying to get a plastic baby to sleep.

OPTIONS

'Hush-a-by baby' is the first line given in the first published version, in *Mother Goose's Melody* (1765). Here's another alternative verse:

> Rock-a-bye, baby, thy cradle is green;
> Father's a nobleman, mother's a queen;
> And Betty's a lady, and wears a gold ring;
> And Johnny's a drummer, and drums for the king.

Rock-a-bye ba - by, on the tree-tops, When the wind blows, the cra-dle will rock,

When the bough breaks, the cra-dle will fall, And down will come ba-by, cra-dle and all.

Rock-a-bye baby, on the treetops,
When the wind blows, the cradle will rock,
When the bough breaks, the cradle will fall,
And down will come baby, cradle and all.

Hush, Little Baby

SINCE MOCKINGBIRDS are from the New World, this is probably an American song, but its date and writer are unknown.

Hush, lit-tle ba-by, don't say a word, Ma-ma's gon-na buy you a mock-ing-bird.

And if that mock-ing-bird don't sing, Ma-ma's gon-na buy you a dia-mond ring.

Hush, little baby, don't say a word,
Mama's gonna buy you a mockingbird.

And if that mockingbird don't sing,
Mama's gonna buy you a diamond ring.

And if that ring it turns brass,
Mama's gonna buy you a looking glass.

And if that looking glass gets broke,
Mama's gonna buy you a billy goat.

And if that billy goat don't pull,
Mama's gonna buy you a cart and bull.

And if that cart and bull turn over,
Mama's gonna buy you a dog named Rover.

And if that dog Rover won't bark,
Mama's gonna buy you a horse and cart.

And if that horse and cart fall down,
You'll still be the prettiest girl in town.

Twinkle, Twinkle, Little Star

THE WORDS OF this English song are by Jane Taylor, whose poem 'The Star' was published in 1806. It's sung to the same tune as 'Ah, Vous dirai-je, Maman' (see 'Baa Baa, Black Sheep', p. 222).

ACTIONS

Red went through a phase of singing this all day long, it being the first song he learned. I've just discovered there are actions to go with it. Are these a new addition or am I slow on the uptake here? Basically, hold up both hands and clench and open your fists, like a star sparkling. At the appropriate moments point up to the sky and make a diamond shape with your fingers. That's it.

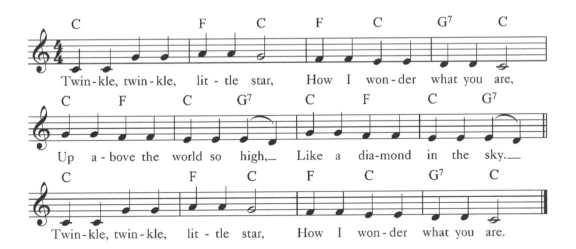

Twinkle, twinkle, little star,
How I wonder what you are,
Up above the world so high,
Like a diamond in the sky.
Twinkle, twinkle, little star,
How I wonder what you are.

When the blazing sun is gone,
When he nothing shines upon,
Then you show your little light,
Twinkle, twinkle, all the night.
Twinkle, twinkle, little star,
How I wonder what you are.

Then the traveller in the dark
Thanks you for your tiny spark,
He could not see which way to go
If you did not twinkle so.
Twinkle, twinkle, little star,
How I wonder what you are.

In the dark blue sky you keep,
And often through my curtains peep,
For you never shut your eye,
'Til the sun is in the sky.
Twinkle, twinkle, little star,
How I wonder what you are.

As your bright and tiny spark
Lights the traveller in the dark,
Though I know not what you are,
Twinkle, twinkle, little star.
Twinkle, twinkle, little star,
How I wonder what you are.

All Through the Night

THE PIANO was always there, and I started banging on it as soon as I realized I could climb up to reach those keys. I loved making up tunes and my mother decided I should get proper lessons. Mr Croot lived across the road, down the steps and past some rough ground and the stream that my dad turned fluorescent green with now-illegal caving dye one winter. And then you went through their shiny metal gate and into the large imposing house overlooking the sea. The bay window is still there, and in my mind's eye Mr Croot is still in it, in his burgundy velvet dressing gown with a gold twisted-rope belt. He always seemed to be in a light snorting sleep till a wrong note was hit, then his paper-dry, nose-scratching fingers would swoop down on mine. He never missed. I missed many notes but he never missed my fingers. But I stayed, and I played. I loved to play there in that bay window for the old fan of tunes like this.

It's a traditional Welsh tune, first recorded in the *Musical and Poetical Relics of the Welsh Bards* (*c.*1784). The Welsh words were written by the prolific poet John Ceiriog Hughes in the nineteenth century. The English version was written by Harold Boulton (1884).

TRANSLATION

'The eyelids of the stars sing all night long. This is the way to glory's country all night long. Any other light is darkness; but showing true beauty is this heavenly family in peace, all night long.'

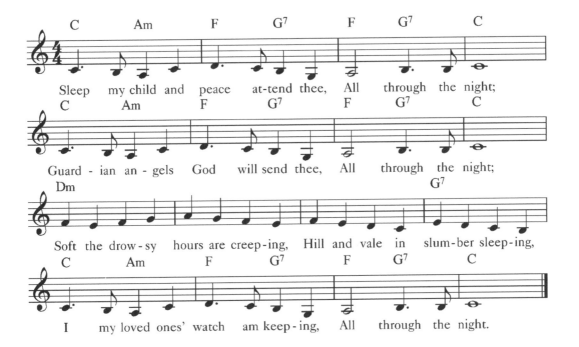

Sleep my child and peace attend thee,
All through the night;
Guardian angels God will send thee,
All through the night;
Soft the drowsy hours are creeping,
Hill and vale in slumber sleeping,
I my loved ones' watch am keeping,
All through the night.

Holl amrantau'r sêr ddywedant
Ar hyd y nos,
Dyma'r ffordd i fro gogoniant
Ar hyd y nos,
Golau arall yw tywyllwch,
I arddangos gwir brydferthwch,
Teulu'r nefoedd mewn tawelwch
Ar hyd y nos.

Greensleeves

THE EARLIEST record of this English folk song was made in 1580, as 'A Newe Northern Dittye of ye Ladye Greene Sleves'. It also appears in Child's ballad collection. An idea persists that the lady in question was a rather promiscuous one, even a lady of the night, because they say the colour green used to denote physical relationships, and the green sleeves may be grass-stained from a recent outdoor rendezvous. Who knows for sure?

Alas, my love, you do me wrong,
To cast me off discourteously.
For I have loved you well and long,
Delighting in your company.

Greensleeves was all my joy,
Greensleeves was my delight,
Greensleeves was my heart of gold,
And who but my lady greensleeves.

Your vows you've broken, like my heart,
Oh, why did you so enrapture me?
Now I remain in a world apart
But my heart remains in captivity.
Chorus

If you intend thus to disdain,
It does the more enrapture me,
And even so, I still remain
A lover in captivity.
Chorus

My men were clothed all in green,
And they did ever wait on thee;
All this was gallant to be seen,
And yet thou wouldst not love me.
Chorus

Thou couldst desire no earthly thing,
But still thou hadst it readily.
Thy music still to play and sing;
And yet thou wouldst not love me.
Chorus

Well, I will pray to God on high
That thou my constancy mayst see,
And that yet once before I die
Thou wilt vouchsafe to love me.
Chorus

Ah, Greensleeves, now farewell, adieu,
To God I pray to prosper thee,
For I am still thy lover true,
Come once again and love me.
Chorus

Lavender's Blue

THIS IS another English folk song, written in the late 1600s; the tune may go back even further. Older versions are not as romantic as this dreamy song suggests and are more to do with tempting a lady friend into bed to love the singer (and his dog), but here are the most widely sung verses.

La - ven - der's blue, *dil - ly, dil - ly,* la - ven - der's green,

When I am king, *dil - ly, dil - ly,* you shall be queen.

Lavender's blue, *dilly, dilly*, lavender's green,
When I am king, *dilly, dilly*, you shall be queen.

Who told you so, *dilly, dilly*, who told you so?
'Twas my own heart, *dilly, dilly*, that told me so.

Call up your men, *dilly, dilly*, set them to work,
Some to the plow, *dilly, dilly*, some to the fork,

Some to make hay, *dilly, dilly*, some to cut corn,
While you and I, *dilly, dilly*, keep ourselves warm.

Lavender's green, *dilly, dilly*, Lavender's blue,
If you love me, *dilly, dilly*, I will love you.

Let the birds sing, *dilly, dilly*, And the lambs play;
We shall be safe, *dilly, dilly*, out of harm's way.

I love to dance, *dilly, dilly*, I love to sing;
When I am queen, *dilly, dilly*, You'll be my king.

Who told me so, *dilly, dilly*, Who told me so?
I told myself, *dilly, dilly*, I told me so.

The Riddle Song

ALSO KNOWN as 'I Gave My Love a Cherry', this traditional English song may originate in the fifteenth century and was often sung as a lullaby. It's related to Child's Ballad 46, 'Captain Wedderburn's Courtship'. Riddles were very popular, and this song travelled with the settlers to the American Appalachians, where I happened to learn it. As a result, I always hear it in the whiny country mountain voice typical of the area, despite the song's English origin. Here are the lyrics (whiny voice optional).

Here's another riddle (from the early 1700s):

As I was going to St Ives,
I met a man with seven wives,
Every wife had seven sacks,
Every sack had seven cats,
Every cat had seven kits,
Kits, cats, sacks, wives,
How many were going to St Ives?

ANSWER

Answer: One. Everyone else was leaving St Ives.

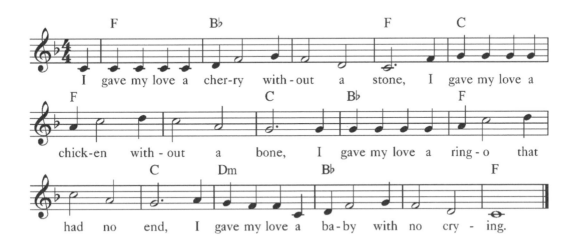

I gave my love a cherry without a stone,
I gave my love a chicken without a bone,
I gave my love a ring-o that had no end,
I gave my love a baby with no crying.

How can there be a cherry that has no stone?
How can there be a chicken that has no bone?
How can there be a ring that has no end?
How can there be a baby with no crying?

A cherry when it's blooming it has no stone,
A chicken when it's peeping, it has no bone,
A ring-o while it's rolling, it has no end,
A baby when it's sleeping, there's no crying.

CHAPTER 11

Christmas and New Year

'Maybe Christmas, the Grinch thought, doesn't come from a store'

~ DR SEUSS

ONE OF MY FAVOURITE CHRISTMAS MOMENTS was when I stood on a chair painting the kitchen wall, watching an old Doris Day film — was it *Don't Eat the Daisies*? *Send Me No Flowers*? I was alone, but that dilapidated mess of a house was filled with a seasonal feeling of hope. I love winter time, real fires being another obsession of mine. I think that (along with singing) sitting around a real fire is one of man's lost soul-feeders. I would much more happily watch flames than television, and often do. I'm not a fire starter in the arsonist sense, though, so no calls to the police. The bit in *A Child's Christmas* by Dylan Thomas where Mrs Protheroe shouts 'FIRE!' and the children throw snowballs and Mr Protheroe slaps at the smoke with his slipper is an absolute favourite to read aloud at this time of year.

Winter brings fires, Christmas, good cheer and good company, or just rest and recuperation, good food and fun songs. Here's a collection of mostly traditional carols — still the best.

Jingle Bells

AMERICAN James Lord Pierpont wrote this song in 1857, and published it as 'One Horse Open Sleigh'. The song was reprinted in 1859 with the revised title of 'Jingle Bells'. Just as you think some songs are old but they turn out to be young, so this comes along, which I'd always presumed was young, written in the mid twentieth century. But it is much older – I was a hundred years out.

Bells were commonly found on horse harnesses' on snow carriages to warn people they were coming, as sleighs were very quiet. It reminds me of the very snowy winter in 1981 when the whole of the UK shut down for what seemed like weeks. You had to walk miles to town for bread, and people helped each other out. It was fun finding objects like old car bonnets or oven trays to act as sledges. Lethal, but they flew down those hills.

Dashing through the snow
In a one-horse open sleigh,
Over the fields we go,
Laughing all the way.
Bells on bobtail ring
Making spirits bright,
What fun it is to ride and sing
A sleighing song tonight!

Ah, jingle bells, jingle bells,
Jingle all the way;
Oh! what fun it is to ride
In a one-horse open sleigh.
Ah, jingle bells, jingle bells,
Jingle all the way;
Oh! what fun it is to ride
In a one-horse open sleigh.

Now the ground is white,
Go it while you're young,
Take the girls tonight
And sing this sleighing song.
Just get a bobtailed bay,
Two forty as his speed,
Hitch him to an open sleigh
And crack! you'll take the lead.
Chorus

Deck the Halls

THIS Welsh traditional song probably dates from medieval times. The lyrics celebrated New Year, but it is now popularly sung at Christmas. The English words are based on those attributed to Thomas Oliphant, published in the 1860s.

Many Welsh folk tunes have 'fa la la la' phrases, like the pub-crawl song 'By Going with Deio to Tywyn', and I usually try and avoid them. I'm afraid of turning into a finger-in-the-ear chin-scratching kind of figure. Here though, fa la la la's are unashamedly sung, because Christmas forgives everything: reindeer sweaters, bobble hats, snowman earrings.

Deck the halls with boughs of hol-ly, *Fa la la la la   la   la   la   la.*

'Tis   the sea-son   to   be   jol-ly, *Fa la la la la   la   la   la   la.*

Don   we now our   gay   ap-pa-rel, *Fa la la   la la la   la   la   la.*

Sing   the an-cient tunes I   ga-ther, *Fa la la la la   la   la   la   la.*

Deck the halls with boughs of holly,
Fa la la la la la la la la.
'Tis the season to be jolly,
Fa la la la la la la la la.
Don we now our gay apparel,
Fa la la la la la la la la.
Sing the ancient tunes I gather,
Fa la la la la la la la la.

See the blazing Yule before us,
Fa la la la la la la la la.
Strike the harp and join the chorus,
Fa la la la la la la la la.
Follow me in merry measure,
Fa la la la la la la la la.
While I tell of yuletide treasure,
Fa la la la la la la la la.

Fast away the old year passes,
Fa la la la la la la la la.
Hail the new, ye lads and lasses!
Fa la la la la la la la la.
Sing we joyous all together,
Fa la la la la la la la la.
Needless of the wind and weather,
Fa la la la la la la la la.

Ding Dong Merrily
on High

THE MELODY of this traditional song first appeared as a secular dance tune in a book by Jehan Tabourot in 1588. The lyrics, first published in 1924, are by priest and poet George Ratcliffe Woodward, whose hobby was bell-ringing (as well as archaic poetry). It's a macaronic song, which flits happily from English to Latin and back again.

I enjoy singing these songs, where the words jump between languages. And yes, the name does come from the same root as the pasta macaroni, so implying that it is like peasant fare, i.e., that this kind of linguistic mash is a tad lowbrow. Here its serious intent and use of Latin may raise its standing, though it's still a macaronic song in my mind.

Ding dong! merrily on high,
In heav'n the bells are ringing:
Ding dong! verily the sky
Is riv'n with angel singing.

Gloria,
Hosanna in excelsis!
Gloria,
Hosanna in excelsis!

E'en so here below, below,
Let steeple bells be swungen,
And '*Io, io, io!*'
By priest and people sungen.
Chorus

Pray you, dutifully prime
Your matin chime, ye ringers;
May you beautifully rime
Your evetime song, ye singers.
Chorus

Little Donkey

WRITTEN BY Sunderland-born songwriter Eric Boswell, Gracie Field's version of this song reached number 20 in the UK charts in 1959. Picture yourself in a studio in June recording all of these songs, with the biggest flight case of instruments, from cabasas to Chinese temple blocks to the humble coconut halves. Pick out the coconut halves and play along, mimicking the gait of this poor little donkey carrying Mary to Bethlehem. What makes donkeys so strong for their relative size? I've always wondered. Mind now, if you could engineer a human-sized ant, donkeys would be out of a job.

Little donkey, little donkey,
On the dusty road,
Got to keep on plodding onwards
With your precious load.

Been a long time, little donkey,
Through the winter's night.
Don't give up now, little donkey,
Bethlehem's in sight.

Ring out those bells tonight,
Bethlehem, Bethlehem.
Follow that star tonight,
Bethlehem, Bethlehem.

Little donkey, little donkey,
Had a heavy day.
Little donkey, carry Mary
Safely on her way.

Little donkey, little donkey,
On the dusty road,
There are wise men waiting for a
Sign to bring them here.
Chorus

Do not falter, little donkey,
There's a star ahead.
It will guide you, little donkey,
To a cattle shed.

O Christmas Tree

THIS IS a traditional German folk tune that, according to the *New Oxford Book of Carols*, first appeared in print in 1799. Older versions of the song contrast the faithful evergreen fir with a faithless lover. The more familiar modern lyrics were written by Ernst Anschutz, a Leipzig organist, teacher and composer, in 1824, and as the custom of Christmas trees developed in the nineteenth century so this song became associated with Christmas.

It has many versions, so I have included a German verse between my favourite English verses. I love singing it, it seems to evoke the best parts of Christmas to me (unless it just appeals to my love of plants) and awakes that inner child.

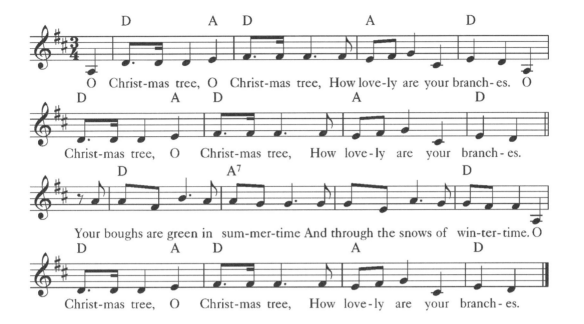

O Christmas tree, O Christmas tree,
How lovely are your branches.
O Christmas tree, O Christmas tree,
How lovely are your branches.
Your boughs are green in summertime
And through the snows of wintertime.
O Christmas tree, O Christmas tree,
How lovely are your branches.

O Tannenbaum, O Tannenbaum,
Wie treu sind deine Blätter!
O Tannenbaum, O Tannenbaum,
Wie treu sind deine Blätter!
Du grünst nicht nur zur Sommerzeit,
Nein, auch im Winter, wenn es schneit.
O Tannenbaum, O Tannenbaum,
Wie treu sind deine Blätter!

O Christmas tree, O Christmas tree,
Your beauty green will teach me,
O Christmas tree, O Christmas tree,
Your beauty green will teach me,
That hope and love will ever be
The way to joy and peace for me.
O Christmas tree, O Christmas tree,
Your beauty green will teach me.

Go, Tell It on the Mountain

ONE OF my top five Christmas songs, this is an African American spiritual and dates back to at least 1865. I've recently recorded it with loads of cymbals and a marching band bass drum (and if you love those big drum sounds, go look for LaVern Baker's 'Saved' for bass drum crazy heaven). It's always best sung at the top of your voice, and be sure to clap on the beat that comes after singing the word 'go', imagining that drum. Punk is not dead! Do not sing this unless you give it every ounce of rebel in you – it's been sung too politely for too long.

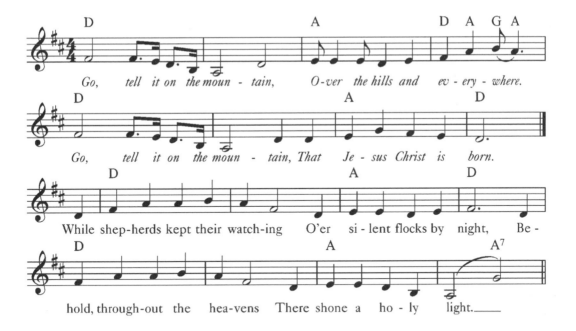

Go, tell it on the mountain, Over the hills and ev-ery-where.
Go, tell it on the moun-tain, That Je-sus Christ is born.
While shep-herds kept their watch-ing O'er si-lent flocks by night, Be-
hold, through-out the hea-vens There shone a ho-ly light.

Go, tell it on the mountain,
Over the hills and everywhere.
Go, tell it on the mountain,
That Jesus Christ is born.

While shepherds kept their watching
O'er silent flocks by night,
Behold, throughout the heavens
There shone a holy light.
Chorus

The shepherds feared and trembled
When lo! above the earth,
Rang out the angels' chorus
That hailed our Saviour's birth.
Chorus

Down in a lowly manger
The humble Christ was born
And brought us God's salvation
That blessed Christmas morn.
Chorus

Away in a Manger

THE WORDS were first published in 1885 in *Little Children's Book for School and Families*, a Lutheran Sunday School book compiled by James R. Murray.

Its author is unknown. The tune most commonly sung was written by William J. Kirkpatrick and first published in 1895.

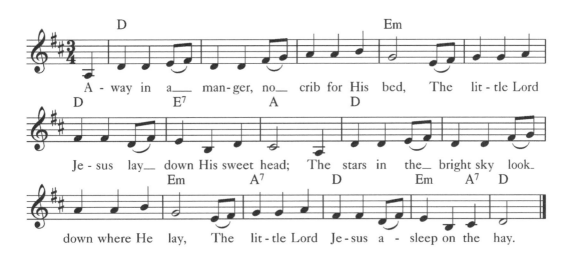

D — A - way in a— man-ger, no— crib for His bed, — Em — The lit - tle Lord

D — E⁷ — A — D — Je - sus lay— down His sweet head; The stars in the— bright sky look—

Em — A⁷ — D — Em — A⁷ D — down where He lay, The lit - tle Lord Je - sus a - sleep on the hay.

Away in a manger, no crib for His bed,
The little Lord Jesus lay down His sweet head;
The stars in the bright sky look down where He lay,
The little Lord Jesus asleep on the hay.

The cattle are lowing, the Baby awakes,
But little Lord Jesus, no crying He makes.
I love Thee, Lord Jesus; look down from the sky
And stay by my side 'til morning is nigh.

Be near me, Lord Jesus; I ask Thee to stay
Close by me for ever and love me, I pray.
Bless all the dear children in Thy tender care
And fit us for Heaven to live with Thee there.

While Shepherds Watched Their Flocks

THE LYRICS (*c.* 1700) are attributed to England's Poet Laureate Nahum Tate, and the melody we sing in the UK has evolved from 'Winchester Old', found in Thomas East's *The Whole Book of Psalmes* (1592). This tune, in its turn, was probably arranged from Cambridgeshire composer Christopher Tye's setting of the Acts of the Apostles in 1553. For me it is the carol most closely related to those memories of the nativity scene where donkeys picked their noses, Joseph cried and Mary waved to Mummy.

OPTION

While shepherds washed their socks by night,
All watching BBC,
The Angel of the Lord came down
And switched to ITV.

Hard not to sing this!

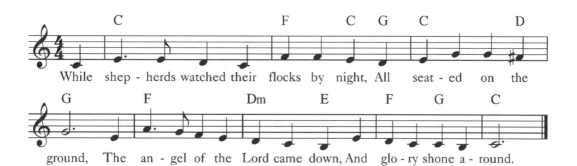

While shepherds watched their flocks by
   night,
All seated on the ground,
The angel of the Lord came down,
And glory shone around.

'Fear not,' said he, for mighty dread
Had seized their troubled mind.
'Glad tidings of great joy I bring
To you and all mankind.

'To you, in David's town, this day
Is born of David's line
A saviour, who is Christ the Lord,
And this shall be the sign.

'The heavenly Babe you there shall find
To human view displayed,
All meanly wrapped in swaddling bands,
And in a manger laid.'

Thus spake the Seraph, and forthwith
Appeared a shining throng
Of Angels praising God and thus,
Addressed their joyful song.

'All glory be to God on high,
And to the Earth be peace;
Good will henceforth from Heaven to men
Begin and never cease!'

The Little Drummer Boy

THIS SONG was written in 1941 by Katherine K. Davis, who may have based it on a Czech carol. Henry Onorati and Harry Simeone were later added to the credits as writers.

It's a poignant song about a poor boy who has nothing material to give, yet he gives what he has: a rhythm, a beat, and so he plays the drum for Jesus. 'And then he smiled at me' – how that simple line touches!

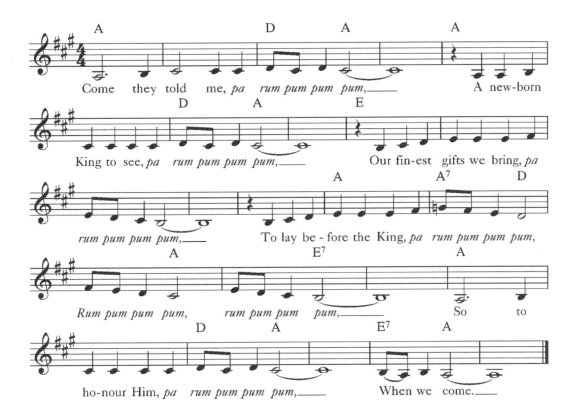

Come they told me, *pa rum pum pum pum*,
A newborn King to see, *pa rum pum pum pum*,
Our finest gifts we bring, *pa rum pum pum pum*,
To lay before the King, *pa rum pum pum pum*,
Rum pum pum pum, rum pum pum pum,
So to honour Him, *pa rum pum pum pum*,
When we come.

Little Baby, *pa rum pum pum pum*,
I am a poor boy too, *pa rum pum pum pum*,
I have no gift to bring, *pa rum pum pum pum*,
That's fit to give a King, *pa rum pum pum pum*,
Rum pum pum pum, rum pum pum pum,
Shall I play for you, *pa rum pum pum pum*,
On my drum?

Mary nodded, *pa rum pum pum pum*,
The ox and lamb kept time, *pa rum pum pum pum*,
I played my drum for him, *pa rum pum pum pum*,
I played my best for him, *pa rum pum pum pum*,
Rum pum pum pum, rum pum pum pum,
And then he smiled at me, *pa rum pum pum pum*,
Me and my drum.

Silent Night

STORES IN America (and more and more in this country too) swing eternally from one celebration to another: Valentine's Day, Easter, Mother's Day, Father's Day, the Fourth of July, Hallowe'en, Thanksgiving, Christmas ... and with this, one must change one's wardrobe. In the American South, for sure, one would *have* to match one's earrings to the season. Pumpkin earrings with autumn-leaf sweater, sledge earrings with snowman gilet – oh, it's a blast! And when the year is over, take them to Goodwill. To go along with these calendar-led outfits, calendar-led musak pumps out from tinny speakers.

At Christmas 'Silent Night', dirge-like and too sweet for belief, would be on heaviest rotation.

I did love the song; it's a beauty. But if I ever came close to having any power? I'd ban musak versions of it being played on telephone waiting lines and in lifts and shops. Ho, ho, ho!

The lyrics were written in 1816 by Austrian priest Joseph Mohr; his friend Franz Xavier Gruber wrote the melody in 1818, on Christmas Eve, so the story goes: the organ of the small alpine village church was broken so the simple score had to be finished in time for midnight mass. The third verse opposite is in Spanish.

Silent night, holy night!
All is calm, all is bright
Round yon Virgin Mother and Child.
Holy Infant so tender and mild,
Sleep in heavenly peace!
Sleep in heavenly peace!

Stille Nacht, heilige Nacht,
Alles schläft; einsam wacht
Nur das traute hochheilige Paar.
Holder Knabe im lockigen Haar,
Schlaf in himmlischer Ruh!
Schlaf in himmlischer Ruh!

Noche de paz, noche de amor,
Todo duerme en derredor.
Entre sus astros que esparcen su luz
Bella anunciando al niñito Jesús.
Brilla la estrella de paz,
Brilla la estrella de paz.

We Three Kings

THIS CAROL was written around 1857 by Rev. John Henry Hopkins, Jr, an author, illustrator, stained-glass-window designer, clergyman and editor.

I recently recorded this accompanied by a Middle Eastern oud, an instrument which came back with the Crusades. It sounds perfect with this very exotic-sounding carol. Add to this a manly vocal as you imitate each 'magus': Melchior, a Persian, Caspar, an Indian, and Balthazar, an Arab (though many Chinese Christians believe that one of the men came from China). Ta daa! You are a king, following that star, at year dot.

'*Magus*', by the way, is ancient Persian for 'priest' but led to the English word 'magic' and other derivatives associated with the occult because they studied astrology. The gifts of the magi had spiritual meanings: myrrh (used as an embalming oil) was a symbol of death, frankincense (an incense) was a symbol of deity, and gold was a symbol of kingship on Earth.

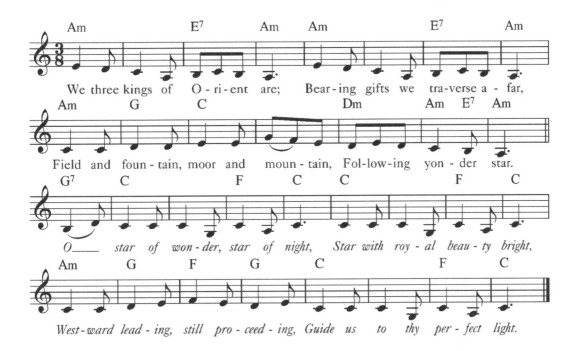

We three kings of Orient are;
Bearing gifts we traverse afar,
Field and fountain, moor and mountain,
Following yonder star.

O star of wonder, star of night,
Star with royal beauty bright,
Westward leading, still proceeding,
Guide us to thy perfect light.

Born a King on Bethlehem's plain;
Gold I bring to crown Him again;
King forever, ceasing never,
Over us all to reign.
Chorus

Frankincense to offer have I;
Incense owns a Deity nigh;
Prayer and praising, voices raising,
Worship Him, God on high.
Chorus

Myrrh is mine; its bitter perfume
Breathes a life of gathering gloom;
Sorrowing, sighing, bleeding, dying,
Sealed in the stone-cold tomb.
Chorus

We Wish You a Merry Christmas

THIS TRADITIONAL sixteenth-century ditty is a great song for those shy about their singing talents – it doesn't matter how badly you sing this; as long as it is done with gusto, it sounds fab. Wealthy people would give treats to carollers on Christmas Eve, which is what this song's all about. And if you're wondering what figgy pudding is, it's basically mashed figs with bread and cream or custard. You can also add butter, sugar, eggs, milk, rum, apple, lemon and orange peel, nuts, cinnamon, cloves, ginger … in other words, it is very much like our modern Christmas pudding.

We wish you a merry Christmas,
We wish you a merry Christmas,
We wish you a merry Christmas,
And a happy New Year.

Good tidings we bring
To you and your kin;
We wish you a merry Christmas,
And a happy New Year.

Now bring us some figgy pudding,
Now bring us some figgy pudding,
Now bring us some figgy pudding,
And bring some out here.
Chorus

For we all like figgy pudding,
For we all like figgy pudding,
We all like figgy pudding,
So bring some out here.
Chorus

And we won't go until we've had some,
No, we won't go until we've had some,
We won't go until we've had some,
So bring some out here!
Chorus

Auld Lang Syne

CALLING all lily-livered cowering beasties who never wait up for the New Year to arrive and are in bed afore midnight – now's your chance to sing. It's generally credited to the great egalitarian Robert Burns, but he was as great a collector and arranger of old verse and songs as he was a writer of original material, and this song already existed in various forms, some dating back to the sixteenth century. Burns added the third and fourth verses in 1788. The phrase 'auld lang syne' literally translates as 'old long since' but what it means is 'the days of yore'. It was the traditional Scots way to begin stories, much as we use 'once upon a time'.

I am a huge fan of Robert Burns, and in 2007 I was delighted to accept an invitation to a Burns supper in Irvine, home to the oldest Burns Club. It was quite a surprise to find out that traditionally it was a male-only club, Burns himself being such a progressive thinker. But things had moved on by the time of my visit, and there were one or two lady members present. It was a splendid evening all told. I learned to pour whisky on my haggis, enjoyed some impeccable performances of Burns's poems, saw Andrew O'Hagan inaugurated by sipping from a ceremonial cup, and I even got to sing 'Ca' the Yowes' to all present. I have put on my own Burns supper for many years, even spreading the word in the heartlands of the American South, flying in frozen haggis from Florida to feed a startled throng. (American import laws forbade a Scottish haggis.)

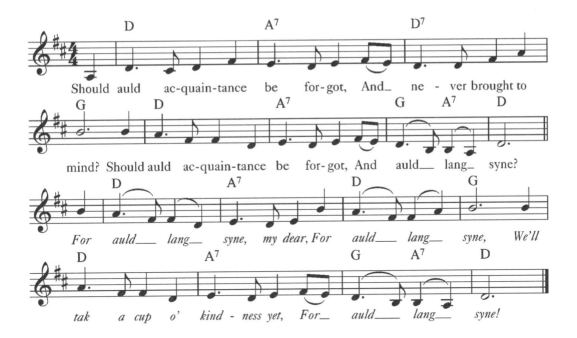

Should auld acquaintance be forgot,
And never brought to mind?
Should auld acquaintance be forgot,
And auld lang syne?

For auld lang syne, my dear,
For auld lang syne,
We'll tak a cup o' kindness yet,
For auld lang syne!

And surely ye'll be your pint' stowp,[1]
And surely I'll be mine!
And we'll tak a cup o' kindness yet,
For auld lang syne!
Chorus

We twa hae run about the braes,[2]
And pu'd the gowans[3] fine,
But we've wander'd mony a weary fit[4]
Sin' auld lang syne.
Chorus

We twa have paidl'd i' the burn[5]
Frae morning sun till dine,[6]
But seas between us braid[7] hae roar'd
Sin' auld lang syne.
Chorus

And there's a hand, my trusty fiere,[8]
And gie's a hand o' thine,[9]
And we'll tak a right guid willie-waught,[10]
For auld lang syne!
Chorus

1. *be your pint stoup*: buy your pint
2. *braes*: hillsides
3. *pu'd the gowans*: pulled the daisies
4. *many a weary fit*: many a weary foot
5. *paidl'd i' the burn*: paddled in the stream
6. *dine*: dinnertime
7. *braid*: broad
8. *fiere*: friend
9. *gie's a hand o'thine*: give me your hand
10. *guid willie-waught*: good draught (of drink)

ACKNOWLEDGEMENTS

Alfred Publishing (UK): 'The Little Drummer Boy' [Katherine Davis / Henry Onorati / Harry Simeone].

Bourne Music: 'Whistle While You Work' [Words by Larry Morey; Music by Frank Churchill] © Copyright 1937 by Bourne Co.; 'When You Wish Upon a Star' [Words by Ned Washington; Music by Leigh Harline] © Copyright 1940 by Bourne Co.

Bucks Music Group: 'Eviva España' [Leo Caerts / Leo Rozenstraten] © Editions Basart Belgium BvBa/ Intersong Basart Publishing Group B.V. (Strengholt Music Group), administered by Bucks Music Group Limited. Used by permission of Strengholt Music Group, Naarden – The Netherlands.

Carlin Music Corporation & Faber Music: 'Istanbul (Not Constantinople)' [Jimmy Kennedy / Nat Simon]; 'Speedy Gonzales' [Buddy Kaye / David Hess / Ethel Lee]; 'K-K-K-Katy' [Geoffrey O'Hara].

EMI Music Publishing: 'The Wizard of Oz' [Words and Music by E.Y. Harburg and Harold Arlen] © 1960, reproduced by permission of EMI Partnership Ltd, London WIF 9LD; 'Pack Up Your Troubles In Your Old Kit Bag' [Words and Music by George H. Powell and Felix Powell] © 1915, reproduced by permission of Francis Day & Hunter Ltd, London WIF 9LD; 'Summer Holiday' [Words and Music by Brian Bennett and Bruce Welch] © 1963, reproduced by permission of EMI Music Publishing Ltd T/A Elm St Music, London WIF 9LD; 'There's a Worm at The Bottom of my Garden' [Words and Music by Jack Martin and Billy Scott-Coomber] © 1952, reproduced by permission of EMI Music Publishing Ltd, London WIF 9LD; 'Over the Rainbow' [Words and Music by E.Y. Harburg and Harold Arlen] © 1938, reproduced by permission of EMI United Partnership Ltd, London WIF 9LD; 'Zip-a-Dee-Doo-Dah' [Ray Gilbert / Allie Wrubel] reproduced by permission of EMI Music Publishing.

Essex Music Group: 'Goodnight, Irene' [Huddie Ledbetter]; 'A Windmill in Old Amsterdam' [Myles Rudge]; 'Little Boxes' [Malvina Reynolds].

Faber Music Ltd: 'Tra La La Song' (from The Banana Splits) [Words and Music by Mark Barkan and Richie Adams] © 1968 Warner-Tamerlane Publishing Corp, USA. Warner/ Chappell North America Ltd, London W6 8BS. Reproduced by permission of Faber Music Ltd. All Rights Reserved; 'I Like Bananas Because They Have No Bones' [Words and Music by Chris Yacich] © 1936 Chappell & Co Inc, USA. Chappell Music Ltd, London W6 8BS. Reproduced by permission of Faber Music Ltd. All Rights Reserved; 'Let's Go Fly A Kite' (from *Mary Poppins*) [Words and Music by Richard M. Sherman and Robert B. Sherman] © 1963 Wonderland Music Company Inc, USA. Warner/ Chappell Artemis Music Ltd, London W6 8BS. Reproduced by permission of Faber Music Ltd. All Rights Reserved; 'Little Donkey' [Words and Music by Eric Boswell] © 1959 Chappell

'A bird does not sing because it has an answer. It sings because it has a song'

CHINESE PROVERB

What's going to work? Team work.

Thanks to Julian Elloway for all-round musical goodness, John Morris at PRS, the team at Penguin: Helen Conford, Georgina Laycock, Rebecca Lee, Patrick Loughran, Emma Horton, Ryan Davies, Hannah Bradbury, Jim Stoddart and Richard Marston.

Thanks to Nick Wetton for clearing of permissions and copyright.

Thanks to Rhys Frampton, Deborah and Golborne Children's Nursery, London, Holly Street Daycare, Nashville, L'ecole Bilingue, London, St Anne's Nursery, London, Miss Shami and St Francis of Assisi School, London, the Frankie Kennedy Winter School, Gweedore, Donegal.

And to: Sharon Radisic, Richard Bennett, Bucky Baxter, Ketchum Secor, Mason Neely and Roy Saer.

Top books over the years: *Soodlum's Irish Ballad Book* (Soodlum Music Co. Ltd), *Mabsant* (Y Lolfa) by Siwsann George and Stuart Brown, *Irish Woman's Songbook* (the Mercer Press), Alan Lomax's *Folk Songs of North America* (Doubleday), *Canu'r Cymru-Detholiad o Ganeuon Gwerin* by Phillis Kinney and Meredydd Evans (Cymdeithas Alawon Gwerin Cymru), Sam Henry's *Songs of the People* (University of Georgia Press) and Iona and Peter Opie's *The Oxford Dictionary of Nursery Rhymes* (Oxford University Press).

Clans: Abbott and Matthews.

And thanks, as always, to the best management duo at Rainbow City — Steven Abbott and Kathryn Nash — and at Eclipse booking agency Wendy Long and Kelly Dillet.

Website: www.cerysmatthews.co.uk
Twitter: @cerysmatthews